T0311705

# Cambridge Elements ≡

Elements in Child Development
edited by
Marc H. Bornstein
*Eunice Kennedy Shriver National Institute of Child Health and Human Development, Bethesda*
*Institute for Fiscal Studies, London*
*UNICEF, New York City*

# COGNITIVE DEVELOPMENT IN INFANCY AND CHILDHOOD

Mary Gauvain
*University of California, Riverside*

CAMBRIDGE
UNIVERSITY PRESS

# CAMBRIDGE
## UNIVERSITY PRESS

University Printing House, Cambridge CB2 8BS, United Kingdom

One Liberty Plaza, 20th Floor, New York, NY 10006, USA

477 Williamstown Road, Port Melbourne, VIC 3207, Australia

314–321, 3rd Floor, Plot 3, Splendor Forum, Jasola District Centre,
New Delhi – 110025, India

103 Penang Road, #05–06/07, Visioncrest Commercial, Singapore 238467

Cambridge University Press is part of the University of Cambridge.

It furthers the University's mission by disseminating knowledge in the pursuit of
education, learning, and research at the highest international levels of excellence.

www.cambridge.org
Information on this title: www.cambridge.org/9781108958127
DOI: 10.1017/9781108955676

First published 2022

*A catalogue record for this publication is available from the British Library.*

ISBN 978-1-108-95812-7 Paperback
ISSN 2632-9948 (online)
ISSN 2632-993X (print)

# Cognitive Development in Infancy and Childhood

Elements in Child Development

DOI: 10.1017/9781108955676
First published online: July 2022

Mary Gauvain
*University of California, Riverside*

**Author for correspondence:** Mary Gauvain, mary.gauvain@ucr.edu

**Abstract:** This Element describes the main theories that guide contemporary research in cognitive development along with research discoveries in several important cognitive abilities: attention, language, social cognition, memory, metacognition and executive function, and problem solving and reasoning. Biological and social contributions are considered side-by-side, and cultural contributions are highlighted. As children participate in social interactions and learn to use cultural symbols and tools to organize and support their thinking, the behaviors and understandings of the social community and the culture more broadly become an integral part of children's thoughts and actions. Culture, the natural ecological setting or habitat of human beings, plays a significant role by providing support and direction for cognitive development. Without the capacity to learn socially, human cognition would be markedly different from what it is today.

**Keywords:** child development, cognitive development, learning, sociocultural theory, childhood

ISBNs: 9781108958127 (PB), 9781108955676 (OC)
ISSNs: 2632-9948 (online), 2632-993X (print)

# Contents

# 1 Introduction

Human beings live in many different environments and have done so for a very long time. The capacity of humans to thrive in various settings is rooted in *cognition*, the mental activity through which we acquire and use knowledge. Cognition includes many mental faculties and processes that enable us to access, examine, retain, use, and communicate information. Put differently, cognition is how we think and what we think about, the ability to solve problems on our own and with others, and the capacity to create, understand, and use symbolic and material resources to support intelligent action.

The knowledge and cognitive skills that a person needs in a particular environment are not present at birth. They emerge and are shaped by the experiences of life. *Cognitive development* is the term used to describe the mental changes that occur as children acquire the knowledge and intellectual skills that enable them to understand and act effectively in everyday life.

In this Element, I describe cognitive development in infancy and childhood. Early life is a period of tremendous cognitive change. Infants and children acquire a vast array of knowledge and cognitive skills, and they learn to use them to guide action. This Element begins by describing the main theories that guide research in cognitive development. Then I turn to the *how* and the *what* of cognitive development. The *how* is about cognitive change over time. In most contemporary theories, cognitive development is seen as emerging from the dynamic interplay of biological factors and experience with the natural, material, and social world. Studies of *what* develops focus on changes over time in mental capacities, knowledge, and skills. This Element describes the development in a wide range of aspects of cognition: attention, language, social cognition, memory, metacognition and executive function, and problem-solving and reasoning.

Cognitive development is simultaneously universal and context-specific. Some cognitive changes are common to all human beings, and others vary within individuals and between groups or populations. This arrangement reflects a hallmark of human cognition – flexibility. People use their mental capabilities to deal with the problems of daily life. Culture, the natural ecological setting or habitat of human beings, plays a significant role by providing support and direction for cognitive development.

## 2 Cognitive Development: Coming to Understand and Act in the World

The world is a complicated place. It is full of objects, some natural and others human-made. It is also full of people and activities. How do children make sense of it all, learn what the world has to offer, and then use this knowledge in productive and satisfying ways? This task, which is already huge, is further complicated because, while children are learning about the world, they are developing in many other ways. They are maturing physically, establishing relationships with the people in their lives, and acquiring and honing a large number of skills that allow them to participate in the activities around them.

Cognitive development is one part of the biological, psychological, and social changes that make up human development. These changes are coordinated with and inform one another over time. They also have contingency relations; changes in one area may enable or facilitate changes in another area. For instance, what children perceive and the objects they explore contribute to cognitive development. Caregiving practices regarding how infants are carried and supported physically affect the development of motor skills along with children's ability to explore and learn about the environment (Karasik et al., 2015).

## 2.1 Internal and External Contributions to Cognitive Development

From early infancy up through childhood, there is a gradual change in children's ability to understand the world around them, learn new information, and participate in activities alone and with others. These changes do not result from a single cause in the organism or a particular experience in the environment (Bronfenbrenner & Morris, 2006). The perspective known as the *developmental systems approach* views development as the product of multiple and continuous bidirectional relations within and between influences internal and external to the organism.

Internal contributions include a brain and neural system that respond adaptively to input from the environment (Lickliter & Honeycutt, 2015). Newborns possess basic sensory abilities that allow them to detect information in the world, rudimentary means for processing this information, and an enormous capacity to learn and learn very quickly (Johnson & de Haan, 2015). This latter feature is especially important because, as children learn, their knowledge and cognitive skills are adapted to the context of growth. Other biological factors that contribute to cognitive development include aspects of temperament and emotion regulation. Psychological characteristics also contribute, including the child's learning history, interests, and forms of self-expression.

As for external forces, a wide range of social, physical, material, and cultural factors contribute to cognitive development. Interpersonal experiences with adults and peers are especially important (Gauvain, 2001). At the cultural level, conventional behaviors, practices, and institutions as well as cultural tools (e.g., literacy, computers) and symbol systems (e.g., language, numeracy) play important roles (Cole, 1996; Goodnow et al., 1995).

The idea that children are active agents in their own development is central to contemporary theory and research in cognitive development (Lerner et al., 2015). Self-initiative in cognitive development is evident in many ways. Children seek out and attend to information that attracts and interests them. When children try to understand something, they use the skills and concepts available to them to carry out goal-directed activities. This is not to say that children are "free agents," so to speak. What children come to know and the cognitive skills they come to possess resonate with the people and environment around them. Children develop knowledge and cognitive skills alongside people who nurture, support, and model understanding and skills, and these behaviors reflect the time and circumstances of growth.

## 2.2 Cognitive Change over Time

In general, the timing and pace of cognitive development are similar for all children. All healthy, full-term human infants have the same perceptual, sensory, and motor capacities at birth. They learn much through manipulating simple objects, observing others, and engaging in activities and social exchanges that are limited in scope and duration. With development, children's abilities to sustain attention, manipulate complicated objects, and participate in complex activities and social interactions expand considerably.

Development is lifelong, and researchers distinguish different types of temporal influences (Baltes, 2006). Age-graded influences are those encountered at particular age points, such as the beginning of school. The timing of these influences varies across social and cultural settings, which affects the pattern of cognitive development (Rogoff, 2003). History-graded influences pertain to specific time periods; they may be culture-specific (e.g., a political epoch or crisis) or widespread (e.g., a global pandemic). Nonnormative influences affect individuals, singularly or in small groups, and can happen at any age (e.g., a severe illness, immigration).

The passage of time is included in developmental theory and research in a number of ways, both qualitative and quantitative, and each has advantages and limitations in understanding cognitive development. The main qualitative approach focuses on mental functioning at different periods or stages of life, such as infancy, early childhood, and middle childhood. Cognitive development is seen as an organized sequence of step-like changes that are qualitatively distinct, build on each other, and affect mental functioning broadly. Most stage theories view stages as common to all species members or universal. Piaget used a stage approach in his theory, described later in this section.

Anthropologist Margaret Mead (1955) also described child development as having several distinct periods that reflect changes in children's physical growth, the settings children occupy, and their experiences and relationships. Mead called infants 0 to 1 year of age *lap children*; next are *knee children*, between ages 2 and 3 years; followed by *yard children*, aged 4 to 5 years; and the oldest group, ages 6 to10, are *community children*. Although this classification does not speak directly to cognitive development, it is relevant to approaches that emphasize social and cultural contributions to mental growth.

Dividing childhood into stages is appealing because it seems to capture the types of changes children go through during development. Yet, on closer inspection, several limitations are apparent. The most problematic is the large span of time covered in each stage, which can overlook cognitive changes within a stage. It is also known that a child can have cognitive skills in one domain that surpass what is typical for their stage, such as musical prodigies, while the child's cognitive skills in other areas are typical for their stage (Feldman & Morelock, 2011).

Chronological age, time since birth, is the most common metric of cognitive development. However, as Kessen (1960) wrote, at every age there are meaningful variations in cognitive performance across individuals and populations. Researchers understand that age does not cause cognitive change, yet age continues to be used in research because in many societies age is the conventional way of describing child development. However, as Rogoff (2003) pointed out, the use of age as a marker of development is relatively recent. It took hold in the early twentieth century in the United States when the scientific study of children was concerned with age-related capacities, referred to as normative patterns (Siegel & White, 1982). Child age was then used to organize children's experiences in school and other settings (Fass, 2007). Since that time, an enormous amount of data about children in relation to age has been collected. Still, relying on age as the main way of describing child development inadvertently decreases knowledge of experiential contributions to cognitive development. As Whiting (1976) explained, age is a social category that represents a "package of information" about a person's lived experiences. When differences are found across age groups, researchers need to "unpack" the information to understand the reasons for the differences.

Experiences associated with age take on additional complexity when cultural factors are taken into account. Cultures differ in their views and beliefs about what children can and are expected to do at particular ages (Harkness & Super, 2020). Even the use of child age as an indicator of development is more common in some cultures than others (Rogoff, 2003). Physical development plays a role, of course, because children's experiences are, in general, related to the biological changes of childhood. Nonetheless, the ages when certain practices and expectations occur in development differ across cultures. Consider the opportunities children have to engage in activities that require independence and responsibility, which foster decision-making and problem-solving skills. In some cultures, 8-year-old children travel long distances on their own to collect water or run errands; in other cultures, children of this same age are not allowed to cross the street alone (Putnick & Bornstein, 2016). In many small-scale traditional societies, children as young as 6 years of age care for younger siblings, whereas in most industrialized societies, this responsibility occurs much later (Lancy, 2008). Cultural experiences also affect how age-related findings can be interpreted. In cultures with compulsory schooling, child age is related to how long the child has attended school. This relation makes it difficult to disentangle which aspects of cognitive development result from increasing age, more years of schooling, or a combination of the two (van de Vijver et al., 2010). In the end, chronological age is not as straightforward a description of cognitive development as it seems.

Another way that research has considered change over time is to examine the path or trajectory of cognitive development. Although it is reasonable to assume that cognitive development undergoes a gradual, linear increase over childhood, this assumption is not borne out by research (Spencer, 2019). Many cognitive functions show this pattern; however, others develop rapidly and reach a stable point, such as the development of color vision in early infancy (Bornstein, 2015). Also, some mental functions decline with time, for example, the detection of certain sound and visual contrasts that are present in early infancy disappear by the end of the first year (Pascalis et al., 2002; Werker & Desjardins, 1995).

The trajectory of cognitive development also depends on an individual's life experiences, especially if (and how) an event occurs that leads to a major shift or transition in the developmental course. Major transitions can occur for any number of reasons: physical changes (e.g., puberty), personal life circumstances (e.g., parent divorce), or a widespread event (e.g., a pandemic). Such occurrences can have different outcomes for individuals depending on a number of factors, which is called multi-finality (Cicchetti & Rogosch, 1996). In longitudinal research on the impact of childcare outside the home on cognitive development, Peisner-Feinberg and colleagues (2001) found that children's reading and mathematics skills in primary school, 6 to 8 years of age, were affected by the quality of child-care when the children were 3 to 4 years old, which was determined by the resources parents had to pay for childcare. The impact of a major transition also depends on when it occurs or developmental timing. An event that transpires over a one-year period may have a different impact on cognitive development if it occurs early as opposed to later in childhood. This question was raised about the disruption to development during the COVID-19 pandemic depending on when in the child's development this event occurred (Bornstein, 2021).

Another way temporality in cognitive development has been approached is through the study of different timescales of change. Timescales range from very brief periods or microgenesis to the lifetime of an individual or ontogenesis, to the trajectory of developmental change, to historical and cultural changes that extend beyond an individual's lifetime (Packer & Cole, 2015).

Microgenesis, which concentrates on learning over a single episode, is limited in what it can describe about cognitive development over longer periods of time (Siegler, 2006). To address this limitation, microanalytic studies often include participants of various ages. Ontogenesis refers to the changes that occur in a lifetime. An ontogenetic study may focus on a short span of time, a few months or years, which is common in studies of young children. Or it may collect information over many years, either on the same individuals in a longitudinal study or on individuals from different age cohorts in a cross-sectional study. Research on longer time spans concentrates on typical or atypical developmental trajectories, such as the project on Environmental Influences on Child Health Outcomes at the National Institutes of Health ; www .nih.gov/echo/about-echo-program). Longer time spans are also examined in research about how cultural or historical changes affect cognitive development. Cognitive development is informed by many aspects of human social life that are passed across generations, such as material resources that support cognition and socially organized activities and institutions through which those resources are transmitted to young people.

In summary, developmental theory and research focus on the temporal aspects of cognitive development in various ways, and each approach offers insight into cognitive change over time. Throughout life, human beings acquire and lose knowledge and skills. Also, the pace of cognitive development varies over time, with more rapid changes very early in life. Some life experiences may cause a major shift in the path or trajectory of cognitive development.

## 2.3 Theories of Cognitive Development

There are four main theoretical approaches to cognitive development. This section describes each approach, along with its role in research and its limitations.

## 2.3.1 Piagetian Theory

Piaget proposed the most well-known theory of cognitive development (Piaget, 1926, 1929). In this theory, cognitive development unfolds in four stages from infancy to adolescence. Each stage is qualitatively distinct, and the type of thinking the child uses at a stage is consistent across areas of mental functioning. The stages build on each other, and the shift from stage to stage represents increasingly adaptive ways of thinking. Piaget viewed cognitive development as an inherent property of human biology, and therefore he considered the stages universal. His is a constructivist view in that knowledge develops through children's activities and efforts to make sense of their experiences. Because the timing of experience can vary across children, Piaget assigned approximate ages for the stages.

Piaget described two processes that regulate cognitive development: organization and adaptation. Organization refers to the sequential structure of mental development from a simple to a more complex system. Adaptation pertains to how developing knowledge matches the environment, and it includes two complementary functions. In assimilation, new information is added to existing knowledge, and in accommodation, existing knowledge is modified to include new information. The purpose of adaptation is to improve alignment between the individual's thinking and the environment, which Piaget called equilibration.

With development, children's thinking changes from a focus on immediate sensory and motor experiences and simple ways of understanding and engaging with the world to more complex and abstract ways of thinking. The four stages focus primarily on logical reasoning; they are the sensorimotor period (0–2 years of age), preoperations (2–6 years of age), concrete operations (6–11 years of age), and formal operations (over 11 years of age). In the sensorimotor stage, thought is based on action and sensory experience, and children change from relying on basic reflexes to learn about the world to being able to think symbolically and carry out goal-directed actions. Many foundational concepts appear including a basic understanding of objects and causality. In the following stages, children's capacity to think logically advances from being partially logical in the preoperational stage, to logical understanding of real or present objects in concrete operations, to formal operations in which the child has the capacity for abstract reasoning.

Piaget's theory stimulated an enormous amount of research, and some of his ideas remain influential, including that development proceeds from early sensorimotor capacities to more complex forms of reasoning (Miller, 2016). However, empirical support for the stages is not strong, especially regarding their age of appearance, coherence across areas of mental functioning, and universality. Infants and children grasp many concepts earlier than Piaget thought (Gopnik et al., 1999). Yet most psychologists agree that Piaget tried to tackle difficult questions and he introduced topics, many of which are at the center of research today such as children's logical and scientific reasoning, understanding of mental states, and concepts of objects and natural forms.

## 2.3.2 Learning Views

The term "learning" has been used in psychology for more than a century. The original conception drew mostly on ideas about behavioral conditioning, but it has been replaced by a focus on how information is processed and cognitive skills are acquired (Siegler, 2005). Learning views concentrate on quantitative change, and the active role of the child is emphasized, including how children attend to information and regulate learning.

A collection of learning views, referred to as the information-processing approach, concentrates on how information flows through the cognitive system and the mental capacities used in these efforts (Munakata, 2006). Studies draw on research conducted with adults in areas such as attention, memory, and problem-solving and aim to determine how and when these mental capacities develop over childhood. With development, the speed, efficiency, and control of information processing improve (Kail, 2007; Zelazo, 2015). This approach is often used to study how children develop knowledge and skills in academic domains (Sawyer, 2014). Cognitive social learning theory broadened this perspective by emphasizing how children learn by observing others (Bandura, 1997).

The field of cognitive developmental neuroscience contributes to the understanding of how learning affects cognitive development by examining changes in neural functioning (Johnson & de Haan, 2015). Repeated activation of neural connections can help integrate established networks, create new networks, and lead to structural changes that reshape behavior (Mareschal et al., 2007). Research has also investigated how experience can expose learners to structured input, or patterns, in the environment that the brain is able to detect and process (Bates & Elman, 1996). For instance, over the first year of life, infants learn language by attending to the patterns of sounds in the speech around them (Saffran et al., 1996).

Research has elucidated connections among brain development, specific learning experiences, and the organization of children's thinking at different points in growth. These studies provide detailed information about learning in specific domains, but they do not embrace cognitive development more generally.

### 2.3.3 Sociocultural Perspectives

The sociocultural approach looks beyond the individual and into the wider social and cultural context to understand cognitive development (Rosa & Valsiner, 2018). In this view, cognitive development emerges from children's interactions with other people and with the activities and objects around them (Gauvain & Perez, 2015). These experiences include the valued knowledge and ways of acting and thinking in the culture in which a child lives.

The sociocultural approach is influenced by the ideas of Vygotsky (1978) who proposed that social and cultural experiences facilitate cognitive development by transforming basic mental functions into more complex forms of cognition through the use of signs and tools of the culture. This transformation occurs through interactions with more experienced cultural members, including caregivers, teachers, and older children. It is a social constructivist view – when children learn from others, they play an active, constructive role in development (Tomasello et al., 2005). Vygotsky's (1978) concept of the zone of proximal development (ZPD), which is the region of sensitivity for learning in a particular domain of knowledge, has been especially influential. When experienced partners provide support, or scaffolding, for learning that is targeted at the child's ZPD, the child is able to use current capabilities to engage in, and eventually adopt, higher levels of competence (Wood et al., 1976).

Sociocultural theorists are interested in the cultural practices and tools that support and extend human thinking, referred to as mediators, and how children come to learn and use them to support thinking (Wertsch, 2007). Vygotsky (1987) considered language an especially important cultural tool because it allows children to communicate with and learn from others. In addition, over development language is increasingly used in an egocentric form, which Vygotsky called private speech, that is self-directed and used to guide behavior.

In the sociocultural approach, relations between culture and individual cognitive development are dynamic and reciprocal (Goodnow, 2010). Culture affects cognitive development because children learn about and practice behaviors that have value and make sense in their cultural setting. Children change cognitively as they adopt the symbolic and material tools of the culture. The culture also changes as children adapt these tools and practices to meet their own needs and interests (Bornstein, 2009; Gauvain, 2009; Greenfield, 2009).

The sociocultural approach has advanced theory and research on cognitive development in several ways. By emphasizing the socially mediated nature of cognitive development, it highlights how social experiences contribute to cognition and offers new ways of assessing children's cognitive potential and of teaching academic subject matter to children (National Academies of

Sciences, Engineering, of Medicine, 2018). This approach has increased appreciation of the importance of culture in cognitive development and provided a theoretical way of understanding cultural variation in cognitive development that is not based on a deficit model. That said, the sociocultural approach to cognitive development is still in a formative stage. Research to date has mainly focused on microgenetic change, and attention to cognitive development across longer time periods is needed.

### 2.3.4 Dynamic Systems

Another theoretical approach, based on dynamic systems theory, views cognitive development as part of a complex, integrated system in which individual behaviors are influenced by other elements of the system (Sameroff, 2009; Thelen & Smith, 2006). The word dynamic is used to underscore the constant interaction and mutual influence of the elements of the system. A key component is self-organization, the idea that development is produced through the interactions of the various elements of the system. The system includes the biological properties of the organism that support development, actions of the organism in using these properties, and input from the environment. Together, these elements produce a set of behaviors that lead to cognitive change.

Dynamic systems theory has been used to study a number of topics in child development. In some research, the focus is on the child alone and how the child, as a biological and psychological system, functions and grows in the physical world that both supports and challenges development (Thelen & Smith, 2006). For example, in learning to walk, infants must coordinate their physical abilities, including muscle strength, balance, and momentum, with features of the physical world such as gravity and the properties of the walking surface. Only when the entire system is coordinated and mastered does the child succeed at walking.

Dynamic systems theory has the potential to integrate many aspects of development into a single, overarching theory (Spencer et al., 2011). However, the complexity of this approach raises questions about its utility in understanding cognitive development (Miller, 2016).

The four main theories of cognitive development are summarized in Table 1. Together, these approaches address many key questions about cognitive development. They consider the contributions of internal and external forces, but they take different positions on how those forces affect cognitive growth. All four theories view the child as an active agent in cognitive development, yet the theories differ in the aspects of cognitive development they try to explain.

**Table 1** Summary of the four main theories of cognitive development

| Theory | Main Focus | Strengths | Limitations |
|---|---|---|---|
| Piagetian theory | Development of cognition over four qualitatively distinct stages from birth to early adolescence considered universal to the species | Insight into characteristic aspects of thinking in infancy and childhood; introduced key research topics including logical, scientific, and mental state reasoning | Weak empirical support for the stages regarding their age of appearance, coherence across areas of mental functioning, and universality |
| Learning views | How information is processed and cognitive skills are acquired and utilized at different ages in infancy and childhood | Detailed descriptions of children's learning in specific domains and of age-related differences in basic cognitive capacities and control of the cognitive system | Insufficient attention to processes that produce cognitive change and to development more generally, interrelations of cognitive capacities unclear |
| Sociocultural perspectives | Contribution of social experiences and aspects of culture to cognitive development | Explains how social experience and cultural practices and tools can support and lead to cognitive development; offers an approach to cultural variation not based on a deficit model | Research mainly focuses on microgenetic changes with little attention to longer time periods, specific connections between culture and cognitive development unclear |
| Dynamic systems | Views cognitive development as part of a complex, integrated system that is influenced by other elements of the system | Emphasis on self-organization in cognitive development; potential to integrate various aspects of development into a single, overarching theory | The complexity of the approach raises questions about its utility for understanding specific aspects of cognitive development and how cognitive change comes about |

Whereas Piagetian theory attempts to describe the universal structure of cognitive development, learning views investigate how specific cognitive abilities emerge. Both sociocultural and dynamic systems perspectives emphasize the role of context in cognitive development, and they attend less to the child's psychological characteristics. In the end, these four approaches concentrate on different aspects of cognitive development, and in this sense, they are complementary not competing views. Finally, each view takes a different approach regarding how development occurs, the topic of the next section.

## 3 Processes and Mechanisms of Cognitive Development

This section is about how cognition develops, the processes and mechanisms that bring about changes in children's thinking. First, a comment on terminology. Both terms – process and mechanism – are used to describe how developmental change occurs. The choice of term reflects the philosophical view of human nature that underlies a developmental theory (Overton, 1984). Researchers who favor the word *process* tend to hold an organismic or biological view, whereas researchers who use *mechanism* tend to endorse an operational view based, metaphorically, on how machines work. Both terms are used in this section, respecting their theoretical frameworks.

Why discuss *how* developmental change occurs? For a theory to be developmental, it must focus on change over time *and* include explanation of how that change occurs (Miller, 2016). Despite its importance to the field, the study of the processes and mechanisms is limited because as Flavell (1984) remarked, it is "very, very hard to do" (p. 198). Since Flavell made this comment, new ways of describing how cognitive development occurs have come to light, and some have upended the mostly implicit maturational explanations that dominated the field for years.

These innovations include better understanding of the biological basis of cognitive development, in particular epigenetic inheritance (Jablonka & Lamb, 2007) and neural development (Mareschal et al., 2007). Sociocultural theory, which emphasizes how the social and cultural context leads cognitive development, has had substantial impact (Packer & Cole, 2015). Most contemporary perspectives to cognitive development incorporate these ideas to some degree and endorse a biologically informed approach that takes experience into account. An important and foundational part of this story, covered next, is the human capacity to develop cognition that emerged over evolution.

### 3.1 The Nature and Nurture of the Human Mind

Cognitive development was shaped over human evolution and involves the coordination of intellectual, social, and emotional adaptations (Bjorklund,

2020). Neurological features, in particular brain flexibility or plasticity, along with the immaturity of the brain at birth, are vital. In addition, human beings have a vast potential for learning, along with a highly social nature and ability to form strong emotional ties. How do these adaptations contribute to cognitive development as human beings experience it today?

The limited physical capacities of the human infant necessitate a lengthy period of dependence on other people along with great parental investment in very few offspring (Konner, 2010). To safeguard the survival of infants and young children, a form of caregiving emerged, one that involves substantial contact with more mature group members. Young species members also have a lot to learn, they are capable of doing so, and their caregivers know much of what children need to know to survive in the environment in which they live. Thus, the form and frequency of early social contact help children survive while at the same time learn about the world immediately around them. Human sociability plays a particularly important role. We cooperate in groups and understand other people in ways that allow us to work together and learn from each other (Tomasello, 2009). Also, our capacity to create strong emotional ties enhances the potential for learning early in life (Hinde, 1989). Deep and abiding affective relationships create a secure base for exploring the world (Bowlby, 1988) and arouse emotions that foster motivation for learning (Heckhaussen, 2000).

Evolution also set in place several tendencies that support the development of social skills that help us learn from others. These tendencies are present early in life and include perceptual preferences for patterns that coincide with human social behavior and orient young infants to social partners. Full-term newborns only 30 minutes of age prefer face-like patterns over patterns that do not have such features (Mondloch et al., 1999), and 2-day-old babies are more interested in the sounds made by the human voice as compared to other sounds (Saffran et al., 2006). Over the first year of life, the infant's visual and auditory systems are increasingly aligned with human social behavior as expressed by those around them (Kellman & Arterberry, 2006; Pascalis et al., 2002).

It is important to appreciate that the infant's apparent social behaviors in the first weeks and months of life are largely controlled reflexively by subcortical visuomotor pathways (Johnson & de Haan, 2015). Over the first months, as the neural system develops, control of cognitive functions shifts to cortical regions, specifically the temporal and occipital lobes. By 2 to 3 months of age, cognitive functions are largely under voluntary control (Nelson et al., 2006). What this means is that the behaviors of very young infants that appear social, such as gazing at or listening to the caregiver, are not deliberate. Rather, they reflect a perceptual bias built into the neural system that, as Johnson (2005, p. 97) explains, is "the minimum necessary for picking out faces from a natural environment." These infant behaviors set in motion experiences crucial to survival, including recognizing caregivers and enlisting them in the enormous amount of care that young babies require. What is also important is that caregivers perceive and respond to the infant's behaviors as genuine social behaviors. These early behaviors provide the child with ready access to learning from people who are emotionally invested in the child.

In summary, cognitive development as experienced by human beings today was shaped over human evolution and relies on the coordination of intellectual, social, and emotional adaptations. It is rooted in our unique neural functioning, great capacity for learning, and particular forms of nurturance and sociability.

## 3.2 Biological and Neural Functioning

Advances in knowledge of genetic transmission and the development of the central nervous system, including brain functioning, have increased understanding of how cognitive abilities emerge over childhood (Johnson, 2011). The field of biology called "epigenetics" investigates the mechanisms that regulate genetic expression (Rutter, 2006; Turkheimer, 2000). Individuals inherit many genes and not all of them are expressed. Genes do not work in isolation from the environment, as Moore (2015, p. 6) put it "our features always arise from both nature and nurture." The challenge for researchers is to understand how these contributions explain the emergence and shape of a particular behavior (Tabery, 2014).

Interactions between genes and the environment produce biochemical changes in the genome that affect brain development and functioning (Meaney, 2010). The theory of probabilistic epigenesis is concerned with the likelihood of a gene being expressed (Gottlieb, 1997). This view posits that genetic outcomes are influenced by multiple and continuous bidirectional associations within and between levels of the developing system. These levels include genetic activity, neural activity, behavior, and the physical, social, and cultural aspects of the environment, as shown in Figure 1 (Gottlieb, 2007). The important point for the present discussion is that complex structures and functions of the organism, including cognitive development, are not predetermined genetically. Genes and the environment mutually influence each other and are part of a larger system that determines developmental outcomes (Gottlieb, 1992; Witherington & Lickliter, 2017).

The field of developmental cognitive neuroscience integrates probabilistic epigenetics with interactions between normal brain development and personal

**Bidirectional influences**

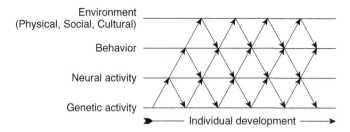

Environment
(Physical, Social, Cultural)

Behavior

Neural activity

Genetic activity

← Individual development →

**Figure 1** Probabalistic-epigenetic framework. This diagram shows the various levels of influence on individual development, from genetic to environmental, broadly construed, and their ongoing and bidirectional relation to each other. From Gottlieb (1992, p. 186). Copyright © 1992 and Imprint. Reprinted with permission from Taylor & Francis Group LLC

experience (Johnson & de Haan, 2015). In this view, neural development is context-dependent and self-organizing. Development builds on preexisting structures and current representations in the neural system, which provide direction and constraints for later development. Because of cumulative effects, early learning is more open to input than later learning (Mareschal et al., 2007). This premise reflects theorizing by Waddington (1962, 1966) regarding canalization and the range of possible developmental outcomes for a genetic trait.

Thus, early learning builds on the architecture of the human brain and the ability of the neural system to self-organize in relation to input from the environment (Johnson & de Haan, 2015). The largest portion of the brain, the cerebrum, is covered by the cerebral cortex, a convoluted layer that is divided into regions whose cells control specific functions such as seeing, hearing, feeling, moving, and thinking. In the first two years of life, neuron proliferation, the formation of nerve cells or neurons, is at very high levels. The number and density of connections between neurons or synapses, which are critical to learning, increase greatly and neural connections that are no longer useful are pruned back. With development, the speed and efficiency with which information is transmitted in the brain increases due to myelination, the formation of a fatty sheath around the axon or nerve fiber that connects neurons. Together, these changes create a responsive and powerful sensory and cognitive system that is actively engaged with the world and ready to learn.

The flexibility or plasticity of the human brain in response to experience is a key component, and two types of experience contribute to brain development (Greenough et al., 1987). Experiences unique to individuals are called "experience-dependent," and universal species-general contributions to brain development are called "experience-expectant." The latter include patterned visual input, touch, affectionate expressions from caregivers, and language processing capabilities. Brain development is affected by both types of experiences, and both can alter genetic expression and neural growth that, in turn, can affect the developmental trajectory. Development is especially influenced by experiences that are forceful and sustained, as is the case for experience-expectant occurrences critical for survival. Experience-dependent occurrences that disrupt normal development, such as ongoing stressors in the rearing system (e.g., maternal depression, chronic malnutrition), can also be forceful and sustained, and when they are they affect further development (Conradt, 2017; Esposito et al., 2017; Hackman et al., 2010).

Alteration of the normal developmental trajectory occurs when experience modifies the neural pathway and constrains further development. Enriched environments that permit a great deal of activity and exploration are related to increases in brain size, number of neural connections, and key brain chemicals. In young children, enriched experience in an area such as musical training leads to more neural connections in related areas (Sarnthein et al., 1997). In contrast, early deprivation, as occurs for children reared in unstimulating and unresponsive environments, can reduce levels of neural connectivity and cortical activity (Van IJzendoorn et al., 2020). Some recovery is possible following deprivation, but the type and timing of treatment or intervention are critical to realigning development.

In summary, new biological approaches to human development are advancing the understanding of cognitive development. These approaches emphasize the bidirectional nature of changes at multiple levels from genes to the physical, social, and cultural environments (Westermann et al., 2007). This research tells us that the contexts of growth provide experiences that affect learning and cognitive development and there is a biological basis for the changes that occur. Accordingly, cognitive and neural changes cannot be understood in isolation from one another or apart from the environment. So how does experience in the environment, especially those that are experience-expectant and critical for survival, become part of cognitive development?

## 3.3 Social and Cultural Contributions to Cognitive Development

From the beginning of life, children are immersed in a social context whose members are deeply committed to caring for them and helping them live successfully in that setting. These individuals are part of a culture, and they ensure that children learn to think and act in ways consistent with the culture. From this vantage point it is easy to see that cognitive development does not happen by the child alone. Rather, it is socially constituted (Packer & Cole, 2015). The child's biological and cultural heritage sets the stage for mental growth and this growth occurs in a rich social setting that is informed by the activities and practices of the cultural group and fortified by emotional connections.

Many and varied types of social experience contribute to cognitive development. These experiences allow for the cultural specialization of cognitive development by transforming children's basic psychological abilities, such as innate perceptual and memory skills, into complex psychological functions tailored to the needs and interests of the group (Vygotsky, 1987; Wertsch, 2007). Consider how human memory is affected by the sociocultural context of development. The basic, involuntary form of memory is composed of images and impressions of entities and events in the environment. Culturally mediated forms of memory use the signs and tools of the culture to support and extend this cognitive capability. The cultural practice of literacy, for example, enables a person to write information on paper, or another mode of storage, with the purpose of remembering the information for later use. Cultural signs and tools, such as literacy, that extend cognitive capacities are transmitted socially across generations. They support and transform human thinking and, in so doing, align it with the thinking of other cultural members and with ancestors (Cole, 1996).

Here I describe four social learning processes of cognitive development, *observing, sharing, transmitting*, and *participating,* through which children come to understand and engage in the world in ways that fit with the people and culture around them. These processes are summarized in Table 2. Although they are not the only social means through which culture affects cognitive development, research has identified them as particularly important (Gauvain & Nicolaides, 2015). These four processes appear to be universal, although their exact form and emphasis differ across cultures (Bornstein, 1995). In cultures with formal schooling, transmission assumes great significance, whereas in cultures with less emphasis on formal schooling children learn much by observing others as they go about their daily lives (Gaskins & Paradise, 2010). Participating and sharing occur in all cultures, although their timing and type, and even the manner in which children engage in them, vary considerably.

*Observing* occurs when children learn by attending closely to the behavior of another person (Bandura, 1989). Learning through observing begins in infancy, and it is a pervasive and powerful force in cognitive development. In observational learning, the learner attends to a model in a nonintrusive manner. Models do not organize or display their behaviors to aid learning; rather, children take active roles by selecting, attending to, and learning the behavior. Given the nature of observational learning, it is restricted to overt behaviors. When

**Table 2** Four social learning processes important to cognitive development from a cultural perspective. From Gauvain and Nicolaides (2015, p. 201).

| Social learning process | Typical focus of learning | Role of learner | Role of other person(s) | Child–other person relationship |
|---|---|---|---|---|
| Observing | Discrete behavior of another person | Observer – selects and attends to another person's behavior and remembers it to use later to meet personal goals | Model – may or may not be aware of being observed | In same physical setting, otherwise need not be related in any way |
| Sharing | Conveying knowledge from one person to another for the purpose of sharing it | Interactive partner – shares knowledge with another or the person with whom knowledge is shared | Interactive partner – shares knowledge with another or the person with whom knowledge is shared | Reciprocal |
| Transmitting | More experienced person teaches less experienced person a skill or understanding | Engaged learner – gradually assumes responsibility for an activity under the tutelage of a more experienced person | Supportive instructor – supports and guides learner and gradually transfers responsibility for the activity to the learner | Learner and teacher |
| Participating | Cultural activity with an identifiable goal and means to reach the goal | Participant – takes part in an authentic cultural activity with the intent to learn about it | Cultural actor – engaged in a cultural activity that is the focus of the learning and provides support for appropriate learner involvement | Inexperienced participant and experienced participant |

children learn behaviors through observation, they store this information in memory and use it later, in the same or a modified behavioral form, to reach their own goals. Researchers distinguish two forms of observational learning: emulation, when learners use their own means to achieve a goal observed in another's actions, and imitation, when learners reproduce observed behaviors to reach the same goal as the model (Tomasello, 2016). Of course, children can only learn behaviors in this way if they have the opportunity to observe them. This constraint makes what is available for learning an important question, one often heard in discussions about what children may be learning when using media in various forms (Wartella et al., 2016).

*Sharing* pertains to situations in which knowledge is conveyed from one person to another for the purpose of mutual understanding. It is reciprocal in that both parties are equal partners, although they may have different capacities defined by developmental status. The purpose in sharing is to involve a person in what another person knows or is thinking about. The information shared and the emotions that accompany it communicate cultural values to children about what knowledge is important and how others feel about it. Sharing is not always initiated by an older or more experienced person, even very young children will point at something to share a sight or a sound with someone else (Tomasello et al., 2007). Sharing begins early in life, 2-month-old infants respond to parental overtures by making sounds similar in pitch to the parent's voice (Snow, 1990), 6-month-olds partake in early turn-taking routines (Bornstein et al., 2015), and later in the first year, infants engage in joint attention when they look reliably at the place where adults are looking (Adamson & Bakeman, 1991). These behaviors are foundational to the development of many cognitive skills, including knowledge about objects, other people, and language. Caregivers and children also share information in conversations about the past and as events unfold that contribute to the development of autobiographical memory (Haden & Ornstein, 2009). The nature of sharing changes with development as children develop social and communicative skills.

*Transmitting* includes social experiences that are intended to pass cultural knowledge on to children. Much of the research on transmitting knowledge focuses on informal instruction and is informed by the notion of the ZPD (Vygotsky, 1978). Cognitive development can advance when children interact with more experienced partners who direct their assistance toward the child's learning needs. Instructional interactions of this type are more common in cultures with formal schooling (Lancy, 2008). Transmission often reflects cultural values and practices regarding long-term goals for children (Gauvain, 2005). Although caregivers and teachers play a central role in transmission, contributions from siblings and peers are also important (Flynn, 2010; Joiner et al., 2000).

*Participating* occurs when children learn about the world and their culture by engaging in everyday activities alongside experienced cultural members (Goodnow et al., 1995). These experiences expose children to cognitive skills and tools, both symbolic and material, that are used in the culture. The child is a full participant in these activities, although the contributions are defined by the child's understanding and interests. Such situations are not designed to teach the child about the culture, but are, instead, done for practical purposes. The authenticity of the activity helps prepare children to become mature cultural members. Children play active roles by directing their attention in an intentional, sustained, and resolute manner toward what they want to learn, which Rogoff and colleagues (2003) called intent community participation. The person doing the activity may assist the child's engagement through guided participation (Rogoff, 1990).

Learnings by participating and by observing are similar, but they differ in several ways. Learning by observing is opportunistic, and what is learned is used to meet the child's own goals, which may differ from those of the model. In contrast, learning by participating in activities involves some awareness of the goal of the activity; if and when the behavior is reproduced the integrity of the activity, including the goal, is enacted. Opportunities to learn through participation change with development, and vary across contexts; for example, children who live in farming communities participate in household activities differently from children who live in urban settings (Lancy, 2008).

These four processes of social learning rely on unique features of developing children, especially their active, learning-oriented nature (Elman et al., 1996). Through these processes, children acquire ways of thinking and acting that coincide with the practices and interests of their culture. Although the processes are described individually, they operate in concert. For example, when children and adults share information, perhaps in storytelling, the adult may also transmit cultural values (e.g., a brief moral lesson) as portrayed in the story (Miller et al., 2012). Social learning provides the child with inroads into cultural–historical forms of knowing and acting, and through them cognitive development finds expression that makes sense to others in their life circumstances.

## 3.4 Changes in How Information Is Acquired and Processed

Over development, the way that children acquire and process information changes. These changes result in a more efficient, effective, and complex cognitive system. Our capacity to process information is limited and, over childhood, several changes come about that improve efficiency and redress the capacity limitations of short-term or working memory, the conscious "workspace" of the mind that includes what a person is currently thinking about (Bjorklund & Causey, 2018). Increased familiarity with routine behaviors and the acquisition of strategies also enhance cognitive processing (Pressley & Hilden, 2006). Many of these changes occur between 5 and 10 years of age and are especially helpful for learning in school (Schneider, 2010).

The way children encode information, which involves selecting and transforming sensory input for more detailed processing, also improves (Cowan et al., 2011). With development, children encode more features of a problem. Duration of attention and ability to attend to relevant information and ignore distractions also improve (Ruff & Rothbart, 1996). Content knowledge expands, and children use it to acquire and organize information (Chi, 1978). Another important set of skills involves control of the cognitive system, referred to as executive function (Müller & Kerns, 2015). This development, especially between 4 and 7 years of age, includes improvement in children's ability to regulate attention and working memory as well as advances in inhibitory control, the ability to hold back a cognitive or behavioral response.

In summary, changes in the brain and neural functioning, input from social and cultural experience, and improvements in cognitive processing all contribute to cognitive development in infancy and childhood. Together, they fundamentally alter how children acquire, organize, and use knowledge. Thus, over a relatively brief span of time, children achieve a remarkably high level of skill at thinking which enables them to understand and engage with the world in increasingly complex and competent ways.

## 4 Acquiring Knowledge and Connecting with the Social World

This section and the one that follows provide an overview of a wide range of aspects of cognitive development. This section focuses on attention, language, and social cognition, which are foundational for acquiring knowledge, a major undertaking in infancy and early childhood. Section 5 covers memory, metacognition and executive function, and problem-solving and reasoning, abilities that expand mental functions considerably. Although the development of these cognitive abilities is described separately from one another, these changes are related to each other and to social and emotional development. To appreciate the profound impact of cognitive development on children and those around them, the changes described here should be seen in a holistic and integrated way.

## 4.1 Attention

Attention involves selecting sensory input for more detailed processing. Attention develops early in life and both the content of what is available to capture children's attention and the way that children learn to use their attentional skills are influenced by the people, things, and activities around them. Sensation, the detection of stimuli by sensory receptors, and perception, the interpretation of sensations to make them meaningful, are integral to the development of attention (Johnson & Hannon, 2015). Research described in this section also includes discoveries in each of these areas.

### *4.1.1 Development of Attention*

From birth to 2 months, attention is reflexive and controlled subcortically (Johnson & de Haan, 2015). At around 2 months of age, there is a shift to more cortical control and subsequent changes occur over the next few years as then other areas of the frontal cortex become involved in attention. The length of time a child can attend to something increases in the first few years of life. Between birth and 2 months of age, infants have very short periods of alertness, and attention is governed by the intensity of a stimulus (e.g., brightness, loudness; Amso & Scerif, 2015). It is worth noting that even fetal and newborn attention is governed by more than stimulus intensity. For example, it is influenced by experience (e.g., Kisilevsky et al., 2003; Swain et al., 1993) and the degree of discrepancy between old and new stimuli (e.g., Weiss et al., 1988).

Although newborns will orient to stimuli, they do so slowly. With more voluntary control of attention around 2 months of age, infants look longer at specific objects or sights, display orienting behaviors such as turning the head and shifting eye gaze, and their visual tracking is smoother. Attention includes more features, such as patterns and shapes, and shifts from external contours of stimuli toward internal features, which aids in processing faces (Maurer & Salapatek, 1976; Ruff & Rothbart, 1996). Consistent with these tendencies, very young infants show some extended looking at faces. Even though young infants are not controlling their attentional focus, when other people interact with them, infants appear to engage in social interaction. The infant's visual tendencies are sufficiently close to those used in social interaction to be interpreted as such by the partner. This type of exchange allows the infant to learn about social interaction by participating in it.

From early infancy, many caregiver–child interactions are about the getting and granting of attention. Infants give cues about their needs and interests to caregivers. These signals are interpreted and responded to in meaningful ways and these experiences can have long-range consequences. Maternal encouragement of infant attention when the infant is 5 months old predicts the child's language comprehension and competence at age 13 months (Tamis-LeMonda & Bornstein, 1989).

At all ages, attention to novelty versus familiarity appears to depend on prior experience (familiarization times, amount of information processed) and stimulus complexity (e.g., see Hunter & Ames, 1988). At 3 to 4 months, other stimulus properties garner attention, including whether an object can be acted on in some way (e.g., touched, grasped; Colombo, 2001). The infant's social looking time also increases, they begin to turn their heads to follow another person's line of vision, and they make eye contact with others in a mutual gaze (Paulus, 2011). Soon thereafter, infants seem aware that their behaviors and that of other people can be related to one another, and infants start to engage in interactions with reciprocity in attention called intersubjectivity (Trevarthen & Aitken, 2001). Through intersubjective experiences, infant attention is socialized, that is infants learn how to pay attention to other social beings. At around 6 months of age, infants engage in turn-taking routines, such as games like peekaboo, in which attention is shared (Bruner & Sherwood, 1976). Between 7 and 10 months, the duration of attention increases and infants are able to look at more distant objects or images. Attention is more flexible, which allows for more rapid engagement and disengagement with stimuli and helps in sharing attention between an object and a person.

How do researchers know what infants are thinking from their attentional behaviors? When infants look longer at one object than another, it is assumed that more cognitive processing is going on. Oakes and Tellinghuisen (1994) found that when 10-month-old infants focus on an object, their behaviors suggest they are concentrating on it compared to when they take a brief look. Infant concentration includes looking directly at the object, changing facial expression while looking, and being less open to distractions.

Another important development is selective attention, the ability to focus on some features of the environment and ignore others (Richards & Anderson, 2004). This ability improves over childhood and provides support for learning. A related development is attentional control, which also contributes to learning. When children are able to exercise control over their attention, they can take in more information and regulate behaviors and emotions that interfere with attentional focus (Ruff & Rothbart, 1996). From 3 to 9 months of age when infants are playing with a toy and a distraction occurs, the infant's resistance to distractors improves. In one study, 10-month-olds were more responsive to distractors (images, sounds) than 26- and 42-month-olds (Ruff & Capozzoli, 2003). Some older children increased their attention to the activity when the distractor was present. This type of responsive attentional control is useful, especially when children begin school and need to focus attention on relevant information when distractors appear (Wetzel et al., 2019). In one study, 5-year-olds in kindergarten classrooms with many wall displays had fewer learning gains than peers in less-distracting classrooms (Fisher et al., 2014).

There are individual differences in how easily learners are distracted by irrelevant information. Some babies can look at or play with a toy for a sustained period, whereas others lose interest quickly and shift attention often (Rothbart & Bates, 2006). These patterns may continue into childhood and in some instances the child may develop a behavioral disorder called "Attention Deficit/Hyperactivity Disorder" or "ADHD." ADHD is characterized by a persistent pattern of inattention, often with high levels of activity and impulsivity. It occurs in 6 percent to 7 percent of children 6 to 10 years of age, and is more common in boys (Willcutt, 2012). The inability to focus attention on the activity often leads to off-task behaviors that can disrupt others. As a result, children with ADHD tend to do poorly in school and are often rejected by peers (Campbell, 2000).

### 4.1.2 Learning by Paying Attention to Other People

At around 12 months of age, infants are able to look reliably toward a place or entity (object, person, event) where another person is looking. This capability allows infants to participate in *joint attention*, the intentional and coordinated engagement between an infant and another person toward a common point of reference (Adamson & Bakeman, 1991).

Between 12 and 18 months of age, infant participation in joint attention increases. By age 18 months, children can direct their gaze competently, discriminate visual targets that are close to one another, and search outside their visual range for an object (Butterworth, 1995). Joint attention is beneficial for learning about objects and other people, including how to direct another person's attention (Carpenter et al., 1998b). Language is increasingly part of joint attention and infants will align the direction of their eye gaze with the mother's gaze when she uses an object label (Baldwin, 1991). During joint attention, adults can either redirect the child's focus of attention, called attention-switching, or follow the child's focus, called attention-following (Akhtar et al., 1991). There are more benefits for language development with attention-following behaviors (Tomasello & Farrar, 1986).

Joint attention is similar across cultural groups, although some differences in communicative style and other practices have been observed (e.g., see Bakeman et al., 1990). A study of mothers and 5-month-old infants in France, Japan, and the United States found the US mothers directed infants' attention to objects more than mothers in the other groups, and US and Japanese mothers had similar, and higher rates, of directing attention to themselves than French mothers did (Bornstein et al., 1991). In research with mothers and 12- to 24-month-old children in a Guatemalan Mayan community and the United States, Mayan dyads attended to several objects simultaneously whereas US dyads attended to one object at a time (Chavajay & Rogoff, 1999).

Late in the first year, infants engage in *social referencing* in which they extract information from a partner about something of shared interest, and then infants use this information to organize their behavior (Feinman, 1992). Social referencing is most common in unfamiliar or ambiguous situations, and it has a developmental course. When infants younger than 9 months of age come into contact with an unfamiliar object or event, they usually stare at it or take some action toward it. At 9 to 10 months of age, infants look at another person to get information and then use this information to guide their response, for instance, if mother's expression toward an object is positive (smiles) the infant moves closer to the object, but if her expression is negative (looks fearful) the infant moves away from the object. Thus, in uncertain circumstances, infants seek information socially and then construct their response based on the information they get – it is not an imitative response.

## 4.2 Language

Language is a communication system in which words and their written symbols are combined in rule-governed ways that make it possible for speakers to produce an infinite number of messages (MacWhinney, 2015). Communication through language is two way: We send messages to others with productive language, and we receive messages using receptive language. Language develops rapidly in early childhood, and it is not solely about learning vocabulary and grammar. Language development also entails learning the sounds of the native language(s) and how to communicate with others appropriately.

Language serves many purposes for the developing child (Hoff, 2015a). It is critical to cognitive development because it helps organize thinking and enables children to express their feelings and ideas. Language helps children guide and control their actions, identify and regulate their emotions, and communicate with and learn from others.

Before infants utter their first word at about 12 months of age, they are involved in preverbal "proto-conversations" with caregivers (Trevarthen, 2002). At 3 or 4 months of age, when someone shows something to an infant, the infant will respond with a smile or gesture (Cameron-Faulkner et al., 2021). At 6 months, infants begin to use pointing to draw someone's attention to something nearby.

Proto-conversations include vocalizations, facial expressions, eye gaze, and physical movement and gestures, along with characteristics of linguistic conversations, such as turn-taking and temporal spacing. Even though caregivers are largely responsible for maintaining the flow of these early conversations, babies behave in ways that encourage a back-and-forth exchange and caregivers respond meaningfully to the infants' vocalizations (Bornstein et al., 2015).

### 4.2.1 How Do Children Acquire Language?

Language is a significant achievement of human development, yet how children acquire language has been a topic of much debate. Theories of language development differ in their emphasis on the contributions of biology and experience. Early nativist views, such as that proposed by linguist Chomsky (1968), stressed biological contributions, claiming that human children are biologically predisposed to acquire language. Evidence such as common structural features across languages (i.e., grammar) and a sensitive period before puberty for achieving native language fluency are used to support this view (Pinker, 2007).

Other early theories emphasized learning, contending that modeling, imitation, and reinforcement determine the likelihood that a feature of language will be learned by a child (Skinner, 1957). Although learning is involved in language development (e.g., vocabulary), aspects of this view are not supported by research. The amount of reinforcement needed to communicate effectively would take longer than it takes children to develop language. This view cannot explain the regular sequence of language development across cultures, that children learn to speak grammatically correctly even though their parents do not reliably reinforce correct grammar, or the creation of novel words by children, such as overextending regular verb forms to irregular verbs (e.g., "goed" instead of "went"; Maslen et al., 2004).

Most contemporary theorists hold an interactivist view of language development in which infants are biologically prepared to develop language through experience with spoken language (Clark, 2019). Social support occurs in many forms, including child-directed speech, with features such as simple sentences and frequent repetitions, and nonverbal games, like peek-a-boo, that teach children about turn-taking (Tamis-LeMonda et al., 2006). Newborns and 4-week-old infants prefer to listen to child-directed speech over adult-directed talk even when it is in a nonnative language (Cooper & Aslin, 1990; Werker et al., 1994).

Cross-cultural research has found that children learn language through various types of social experience including direct instruction, conversational interactions, and by hearing other people talk (Akhtar et al., 2019; Brown & Gaskins, 2014; Fitneva & Matsui, 2015; Ochs & Schieffelin, 2016). What is required to learn language is that children are part of a community in which people interact and talk with one another. With development, children the world over learn much about language, including the sounds, meaning, structure, and use of language.

### 4.2.2 Phonology: The Sounds of Language

Phonology is concerned with the sounds of language, such as pronunciation, intonation, and dialects and accents. There are, on average, 24 consonant sounds in languages, although some languages have fewer – Rotokas, spoken in Papua New Guinea, has six, and some languages have more – some dialects of Khoisan, spoken in Botswana and Namibia, have around 122 consonant sounds including several types of clicks (Maddieson, 2005). Children between 6 and 9 years of age the world over can pronounce the sounds of their language correctly most of the time (Kent, 2005).

Children's interest in and perception of linguistic sounds are evident before they can speak. At 3 months, infants prefer the sounds of human speech versus other natural sounds (e.g., environmental or animal sounds; Shultz & Vouloumanos, 2010). By 8 months, infants extract frequency and contiguity information in speech and recognize and remember groupings of sounds that resemble words (e.g., the first syllable is always followed by a certain second syllable; Aslin & Newport, 2012; Saffran et al., 1996). Over the first year, the ability to distinguish phonemes becomes specialized to the sounds of the native language and infants lose the ability to distinguish the sounds of languages to which they have not been exposed (Werker et al., 2007).

Infants produce many sounds to communicate with other people. At birth, babies cry to communicate distress. One-month-olds will coo, a string of vowel-like sounds. Cooing occurs more often when infants are interacting with caregivers than when they are alone. Babbling, a string of consonant and vowel sounds, begins around 6 months of age. It is not clear that babbling is intended to be communicative because babies babble in many situations, even when they are alone, and they do not seem to expect a reply to their babbling.

Around age 8 months, babies make pre-speech sounds. Like babbling, these are single syllables, but the range of sounds is greater and they are less repeated and more varied (Hoff, 2015a). Infants also start to display the rhythm and intonation patterns of speech, called prosody, of their native language. The sounds infants produce mirror the frequency of these sounds in their native language. The difficulty of producing a sound also contributes to onset age. By age 3, isiXhosa-speaking children in South Africa have mastered most of the sounds of this language, but it is not until age 4 or 5 that children can make most of the click sounds used (Maphalala et al., 2014). The various features of babies' pre-speech sounds help promote early communicative interactions with caregivers (Kuhl, 2009). With development, children also learn other phonetic aspects of their language, such as the appropriate pitch and tone for speaking with different people (e.g., peers or elders; at home, school, or play).

### 4.2.3 Semantics: The Meaning of Words and Sentences

Over the first 5 years of life, children's knowledge of the meaning of words and sentences, or semantics, increases greatly (Parrish-Morris et al., 2013). Children usually say their first words between 10 and 15 months of age, by age 2 they know about 900 words, and by age 6 they know around 8,000 words (Fenson et al., 1994). Social experience contributes to word learning; for instance, the amount of time parents read to their 2-year-olds is positively related to children's language skills at age 4 (Reese, 2019).

Learning the meaning of words is aided by the aptitude children have to assign, or map, meaning to words. When children hear a new word just once, they begin to develop ideas about what it means, which Carey (1978) calls *fast mapping*. How do children figure out what a word is referring to if there are multiple possible interpretations in a situation? Children are guided by several lexical principles or constraints for learning new words (Markman, 2014). The most basic is the *principle of reference,* the understanding that words refer to something, such as an object, person, event, or idea. Also, children as young as 18 months of age, will, on hearing a new word, assume it refers to an entire object, not its parts, which is called the *whole object constraint.* For example, when visiting the zoo and hearing the word "giraffe" for the first time, children assume it refers to the animal and not its neck, height, or coloring. Another language learning principle is the *mutual exclusivity bias*: when first hearing a name or label of something, the child assumes it pertains to a new entity (e.g., object, person) and not a familiar one. This bias is illustrated in a study in which four objects, three familiar (shoe, ball, keys) and one unfamiliar (tea strainer), were put before 28-month-old children (Golinkoff et al., 1992). When asked to give the "glorp" to the experimenter, children handed her the tea strainer.

Nouns are usually learned earlier than verbs (e.g., Bornstein et al., 2004). Within verbs, 2-year-olds are better at learning words for actions they can do (e.g., walk) than actions they cannot yet do (e.g., skip; Huttenlocher et al., 1987). Whether nouns or verbs dominate a child's vocabulary, or lexicon, varies by language. Whereas nouns tend to dominate the first words of English- and Italian-speaking children, children learning to speak Mandarin use equal numbers of verbs and nouns or more verbs (Tardif et al., 1997). The patterns reflect both structural differences among languages and differential emphases by caregivers on nouns versus verbs when conversing with young children (Hoff, 2015a).

### 4.2.4 Grammar: The Structure of Language

Grammar, the structure of language, has two parts: morphology and syntax. Morphology pertains to the smallest structural units of meaning, such as prefixes and suffixes, and how they are used to alter root words (e.g., plurals, past tense). Syntax concerns how words are combined in sentences, such as rules for arranging subject and object, and how grammatical relations are expressed in statements, questions, and so forth.

One-year-old children will express a complete thought by using a single word as a statement, called a holophrase. For example, a child may point at an object and say "down" if they want someone to give them an object beyond reach. Between ages 1 and 2, children put two words together in a statement form called telegraphic speech that uses nouns and verbs but omits other parts of speech such as articles and prepositions. At 2 to 3 years of age, children begin to use pronouns and various verb forms (present and past tense). Most languages combine words in sentences as subject–verb–object, but in some languages these word types can be in any order and young children's syntax reflects these patterns (Hyams & Orfitelli, 2018). At this age, children's sentences become more complex and children begin to ask questions and produce negative statements (Austin et al., 2014; Butler et al., 2020). Between ages 3 and 4, children begin to use forms of the verb *to be* in statements, such as *The book is on the desk* (Budwig, 1990). They also produce more complex sentences such as ones with subordinate clauses (e.g., I want to play with Ben because he is nice.). The syntactic complexity of caregiver speech to young children predicts greater variety in children's syntax later in development (Huttenlocher et al., 2010).

### 4.2.5 Pragmatics: Communicative Language Use

The set of social rules for using language is called pragmatics. Children need to learn how to communicate in ways that are appropriate in the setting in which they live (Ochs & Schieffelin, 2016). Communicative competence includes taking turns when speaking with someone, remaining silent while others speak, and modifying speech in different settings (e.g., more quietly indoors than outdoors) and with different partners (e.g., asking an elder for help is different from asking a peer; Falkum, 2019).

Children display pragmatic behaviors very early. By age 2, they already know how to engage the attention of and respond to a listener and they adjust their speech when talking with children of different ages. Two- to three-year-olds use more repetitions and attention-getting words (e.g., "look," "listen") with younger siblings than with mothers (Dunn, 2002). When playing outdoors, children adjust their vocalizations to the circumstances (e.g., how far they are from others; Göncü et al., 2007). Three-year-olds use different speech registers (types of speech) in different situations and different levels of formality depending on their interlocutor (Sterponi, 2010).

In many cultures, children are taught respectful communication such as when to use polite words and phrases ("please," "thank you"; Ninio & Snow, 1999). They also learn appropriate language use by listening to others converse and by being in conversations (Akhtar et al., 2019; Burdelski, 2010). Children's skill at requesting help is a case in point. Before age 3, children's requests are usually expressed with direct commands (e.g., "Give me the [toy] car."), need statements (e.g., "I need the car."), blunt questions (e.g., "Would you give me the car?"), and on occasion indirect directives (e.g., "I like the blue car the most."; Ervin-Tripp, 1996). Between ages 3 and 4, children's requests incorporate more social factors, such as the status of the listener or interpersonal concerns. They use less-direct requests with people of higher status (e.g., teacher or doctor) or when they are trying to be polite. There are cultural differences in the form and frequency of children's requests. Japanese culture has an elaborate system of polite language and demeanor that even young children are expected to use (Nakamura, 2001).

Children also need to learn how to be effective communicators, including how to evaluate their own speech and that of others for clarity and usefulness and how to listen and respond appropriately. Children develop many of these skills by age 4; however, they are better at speaking in one-on-one conversations than in larger gatherings when they must find a turn to speak (Ervin-Tripp, 1996).

The rules of pragmatics extend beyond spoken language. In all cultures nonverbal communication, such as gesturing, is important for children to learn (Goldin-Meadows, 2015). Very young children use gestures to convey their interests and needs before they can do so verbally, as when infants reach out their arms to be picked up. Infants 12 months of age will point at objects or events they find interesting. If this gesture is responded to by naming the object or handing it to the infant, children learn that the gesture can be used to gather information or regulate the behaviors of others (Callaghan et al., 2011; Liszkowski et al., 2012). Between 6 and 36 months of age, children's use of gestures to communicate increases (Kwon et al., 2018).

Language develops in concert with other capacities. Near the end of the first year when infants begin to walk, there is an increase in caregiver-infant communication that includes action verbs (Schneider & Iverson, 2021). There are also connections between language development and emotional expressiveness, two important forms of communication for young children. Longitudinal research with toddlers 15 to 30 months of age shows a relation between the onset of productive language and emotional expression (Kubicek & Emde, 2012). Early talkers expressed more positive emotions (joy, pleasure) than late talkers, who expressed more negative emotions (anger, fear). Subsequent research with toddlers (18 months of age) and their parents found that children's expression of positive emotions is related to more frequent responses from caregivers (Fields-Olivieri et al., 2020). These findings suggest that child emotional expressiveness may affect the amount of parent–child conversation, which has implications for the pace of language development and also the emotional content of children's speech.

### 4.2.6 Bilingualism

Many children learn to speak two languages, either at the same time or sequentially (De Houwer, 2021). An important factor in how well children come to master two languages is the amount of exposure they have to each language. Very few children who learn Spanish and English at the same time are exposed to equal inputs of Spanish and English (Pearson et al., 1997). Children who had less than 25 percent of their language input in Spanish were unlikely to become competent Spanish speakers.

The effects of bilingualism on children's language learning and cognitive development are of great interest to researchers. Some experts are concerned that learning two languages hinders children's ability to learn language, but research does not support this view (Holowka et al., 2002). Other researchers contend that learning two languages benefits cognitive development by enhancing flexibility of thought and attentional control (Bialystok, 2015). Research results are mixed; when benefits are found, they are relatively modest and it is unclear what produced the cognitive advantage (Dick et al., 2019; Yu et al., 2021). It is unknown whether children who are successful at learning multiple languages are representative of the child population or if they are a select group (Diaz, 1983). We also do not know how many children try to learn several languages but do not become competent bilinguals. The amount and quality of language exposure in both languages are important factors (Hoff, 2015b, 2018).

There is also variation across families because parents speak to children in different amounts and in different ways.

## 4.3 Social Cognition

Social cognition is the aspect of cognitive development about the human capacity to engage with, understand, and learn from others (Carpendale & Lewis, 2021). It encompasses a range of cognitive and social skills including social understanding and reasoning about mental states and behavioral intentions (Homer & Tamis-LeMonda, 2012). Social cognition is fundamental to cognitive development. It provides children with understanding of and access to the thinking of other people along with the ability to share experiences with others and learn from them. Social cognition develops through the interaction of innate biological tendencies and experiences in social context.

### 4.3.1 The Social Brain

The human brain is specialized to gather information about other human beings (Johnson & de Haan, 2015). Brain functions present at birth underlie the ability to engage with the social world and postnatal experiences create the neural connections used to process social information. Infant sensitivity to face-like patterns, described earlier, leads to interactive experiences with caregivers that build cortical areas and neural pathways relevant to social cognition (de Haan, 2008). A related development is gaze detection, the capacity to perceive, monitor, and process information about the looking behaviors of another person (Brooks & Meltzoff, 2014). This capacity appears around 3 or 4 months of age and is well-honed by 5 months. It results from the interaction of emerging brain functions, neural connections, and experience with direct eye contact (Farroni et al., 2002).

Another aspect of the social brain is detection of human action. Three-month-old infants are more responsive to the natural motion of a moving figure, tested with a point-light display showing a person walking, than random movements (Arterberry & Bornstein, 2001). Five-month-old infants can distinguish whether a person's movement (running, walking, kicking a ball in a point-light display) is regular or has been scrambled (Marshall & Shipley, 2009).

### 4.3.2 The Development of Social Cognition

Children develop many cognitive capabilities that help them participate in social behaviors (Carpendale et al., 2018). These capabilities include self-awareness, mental state reasoning, and cooperating and sharing resources.

Self-awareness includes understanding that the self is separate from other people and the surrounding environment. It is fundamental to social cognition because it enables children to develop thoughts and beliefs about themselves, other people, and the social world more generally. Early research using a mirror recognition task found that babies as young as 18 weeks of age will gaze with interest at themselves in a mirror, but they seem to believe that the reflection is another child because the infants sometimes touch the image in the mirror or look behind it for the other child. Research using this approach (by surreptitiously placing a spot of rouge on the child's face before looking at the mirror) suggests that it is not until 18 months of age that children realize they are looking at a reflection of themselves (Lewis & Brooks-Gunn, 1979). However, Rochat and Zahavi (2011) maintain that mirror self-experience presents perceptual and affective difficulties, especially for young children, and that other research indicates that self-awareness emerges gradually over the first two years of life (Rochat, 2015).

Early signs of the development of self-awareness are also evident in interactions between infants and caregivers. At 2 months of age, babies get distressed when their mothers behave differently than their expectations. This reaction is observed with the still-face paradigm in which a mother, when interacting with her infant, displays either a normal expression or an expressionless (still) face (e.g., Tronick et al., 1978). Young infants get distressed during the still-face sequences and exhibit coping behaviors such as smiling less, staring fixedly at mother, kicking fussily, and self-soothing (Manian & Bornstein, 2009). These reactions suggest that infants expect caregivers to behave in certain ways and imply that infants distinguish between the self and the other. Observations of 4-month-old infants support this interpretation. When babies were shown a mirror image of themselves alongside a reflection of someone imitating the babies' actions, the infants looked longer at the image of the person, which (on the basis of infants' preference for novelty) suggests they distinguished that person from themselves (Rochat & Striano, 2002).

Researchers have studied how infants' developing sense of self contributes to shared social activity. Brownell and colleagues (Brownell & Carriger, 1990; Brownell et al. 2006) observed children 12 to 30 months of age as they interacted with same-age peers on problem-solving activities that required cooperation to reach a goal (e.g., pushing a lever to put small toys in a cup). The researchers also independently assessed children's ability to distinguish themselves from others as causal agents. None of the 12-month-olds coordinated their actions or solved the problems; 18-month-olds coordinated their actions somewhat and solved some problems; all of the 24- and 30-month-olds coordinated their actions and solved the problems. Children's ability to differentiate themselves from others as causal agents was positively related to cooperation on the task. It seems that later in the second year of life, children can initiate and manage social interactions to reach a shared goal.

With further development, more complex social understanding appears, including knowledge of mental entities and states (Wellman, 2017). Knowledge of mental entities includes understanding that thoughts about entities are different from the entities themselves and that an object can be something other than what it appears to be (e.g., a sponge that looks like a rock is still a sponge), known as the appearance-reality distinction (Flavell et al., 1983). With this understanding, fantasy and pretend play take on new meaning (Lillard, 2015), and children have ways of coping with situations they find fearful (Sayfan & Lagattuta, 2009).

Over early childhood, children's understanding of mental states changes. In late infancy, children begin to show intentional understanding. In one study, 14- to 18-month-olds were observed as they watched an adult carry out multi-step actions (e.g., an adult holds a wooden box, pulls up a handle, spins a wheel, and a toy appears; Carpenter et al., 1998a). Two types of actions were shown, intentional actions, marked by the adult saying "There!" when completing the action, and accidental actions, marked by the adult saying "Whoops!" Later, when given the chance to imitate the actions, infants imitated almost twice as many of the intentional actions. Another study had similar results with 14-month-olds (Gergely et al., 2002). Infants watched a model carry out an action (turning on a light) with her forehead. For some infants the model's hands were free and, therefore, available to do the action, and for other infants the model's hands were wrapped in a blanket and not available. Most infants (69 percent) who saw the model whose hands were free imitated her behavior; only 21 percent of the infants who saw the model whose hands were occupied used their foreheads to turn on the light.

Much of the research on children's understanding of mental states has used a false-belief task in which children are told a story and then they are asked to make predictions about what the child in the story thinks (Wimmer & Perner, 1983). For example, a boy puts something (e.g., candy) in a particular place (e.g., cupboard) and then goes out to play. When he is playing, his mother moves the item to another location (e.g., a drawer), and later the boy returns and looks for it. The researcher then asks the child where the boy will look. Children 4 to 5 years of age say the boy will search in the place where he put it, attributing a belief, or mental state, to the boy that is different from the child's own knowledge of where the item is. In contrast, 3-year-olds say the boy will look in the drawer where his mother put it; they are unable to separate their own knowledge and the mental state of the boy in the story. These results have been replicated in numerous studies across cultural settings and suggest that age 4 marks a shift in children's understanding of other people's minds (Callaghan et al., 2005; Wellman, 2006).

This conclusion has been challenged on the basis that the task is too difficult for younger children because it requires explicit reporting of one's thoughts (Scott & Baillargeon, 2017). Research with younger children uses a violation-of-expectation task that taps into the infant's tendency to look longer at situations that surprise them (e.g., the location of a toy they had seen hidden elsewhere). On this task, infants as young as 15 months of age behave in ways that suggest they think the experimenter looking for the toy has a false belief about its location (Onishi & Baillargeon, 2005). This evidence suggests that children younger than age 3 have an implicit understanding that other people have mental states (Baillargeon et al., 2016). Implicit understanding in this context means that infants are not consciously aware of the reasoning underlying their behavior, but they have some false-belief understanding that they use to control their actions (Vierkant, 2012).

Between 3 and 5 years of age, children's understanding of their own mental state also changes (Gopnik & Astington, 1988). This understanding is assessed with a version of the false belief task in which children are asked about their own thoughts (e.g., "Where do you think the candy is?"). Three-year-olds answer this question incorrectly, 5-year-olds answer it correctly, and 4-year-olds have mixed responses.

The development of mental states reasoning does not end in early childhood. Between 6 and 8 years of age, children understand that some-one cannot pretend to be something they have never seen or heard of before (e.g., that a character in a story who has never heard of a rabbit can try to jump like a rabbit; Richert & Lillard, 2002). The ability to reason about even more complex mental state relations develops still later in childhood (e.g., Andy thinks that Jen knows that Andy knows that his father wants a hat for his birthday; Liddle & Nettle, 2006).

Children's understanding of psychological states has also been studied by looking at children's evaluation of the actions of others. Six- and ten-month-old infants watched scenarios with different characters (wooden blocks with googly eyes) as they interacted in a video display (Hamlin et al., 2007). In one scenario, a red block was trying to climb the hill but failing and a yellow block, the helper, came along and pushed the red block up the hill. In another scenario, a blue block, the hinderer, came along and pushed the red block down the hill. After watching the scenarios, the researchers tested the infants' attitudes toward the helper and hinderer. Both age groups of infants reached for the yellow helper block to play with instead of the blue hinderer block. It appears that at 6 months of age, infants are already making evaluations of actors in terms of how they treat others, and this knowledge influences infants' interest in the actors.

Children's understanding of the dispositions of other people has also been studied by observing children's reactions to testimony from others. The word testimony refers to statements, written or spoken, that convey a person's thoughts, beliefs, point of view, or understanding (Harris et al., 2018). Testimony is important for cognitive development because what people hear from others makes up a large portion of what we know. The reason is simple – it would be impossible for children, or for anyone, to learn all that needs to be known through first-hand experience. Instead, we rely on or trust information from others.

Research has investigated the types of informants that children find trustworthy. Four- to 5-year-olds tend to endorse new information more readily from their mother as compared to a stranger and from people who have characteristics similar to them, such as gender and age (Corriveau et al., 2009). Children also learn about informants by observing them. In one study, 4- and 5-year-old children watched puppets label several common objects (e.g., book, ball), sometimes the labels were accurate and sometimes they were not (Brosseau-Liard & Birch, 2011). Afterward, the puppets looked in another box containing a toy and provided novel labels for the toy. Later, when children were asked what toy was inside the box, they were more likely to use the label provided by the puppet who had previously labeled common objects correctly. It seems children notice whether someone is telling the truth and they use that information to decide how trustworthy an informant is. Children are not fixed in their judgments, however. Children 4 to 7 years of age will update their views of informants based on changing information about them (Ronfard & Lane, 2018).

Social cognitive capabilities are instrumental to learning and cognitive development. The ability to understand other human beings as thinking intentional agents has profound effects on children's ability to interact with and learn from others. Such understanding also has implications for the development of socially significant behaviors such as empathy, trust, and morality (Cowell et al., 2019; Koenig et al., 2021; Tomasello, 2019).

## 5 Developing and Using the Cognitive System

This section focuses on memory, metacognition and executive function, and problem-solving and reasoning. These cognitive capabilities emerge in infancy and continue to develop throughout early and middle childhood.

## 5.1 Memory

Memory has been a topic of study in psychology since the late 1800s (Schneider & Ornstein, 2015). There are several different types of memory with distinct neurological bases, they are affected differently by experience and have their own developmental course.

### 5.1.1 The Memory System

Models of the memory system describe what happens when we encounter information in the environment, examine it in consciousness, and store it for later use. A leading approach, called the multistore model, describes memory as a sequence of steps for acquiring and storing information (Atkinson & Shiffrin, 1968). We acquire information from the environment through our senses and the information is held for a fraction of a second in the sensory register in a manner close to its perceptual form (e.g., images are stored visually, sounds are stored aurally; Sperling, 1960). If the input grabs our attention, it is examined further in short-term or working memory.

Short-term or working memory (STWM) is the conscious "workspace" of the mind – its contents are what a person is currently thinking about (Bjorklund & Causey, 2018). STWM is limited in the amount of information it can hold; without active effort to retain it (e.g., rehearsal), information is lost in fifteen to thirty seconds (Peterson & Peterson, 1959). The amount of information that can be held in STWM changes with development. Early changes in STWM capacity were examined by showing infants objects on a screen, some of which changed from one moment to the next (Ross-Sheehy et al., 2003). Early in the first year, infants remembered only one item, but by the end of the first year, they remembered four items, which is close to adult performance. Input from the environment is not the only type of information in STWM, information from long-term memory can be activated in consciousness (Cowan, 2014).

Long-term memory (LTM) is the knowledge base, it contains a vast amount of information, and it is separated into declarative and nondeclarative memories which have different neural substrates and patterns of development (Johnson & de Haan, 2015; Squire, 1992). We have conscious access to declarative memory, which is further divided into semantic and episodic memory (Tulving, 1987). Semantic memory includes all the world knowledge and facts a person has (e.g., vocabulary). Episodic memory contains information about specific events and experiences, much of which is autobiographical in nature. Nondeclarative memory, also called procedural memory, includes information such as motor skills (e.g., how to climb stairs) and does not depend on conscious awareness.

LTM changes substantially in the first two years of life as the knowledge base increases (Lukowski & Bauer, 2014). Although it is difficult to assess LTM with pre-verbal infants, over the last several decades, research in this area has advanced with several innovative methods that use recognition, conditioned learning, and deferred imitation. Research using recognition techniques has discovered that neonates recognize a previously experienced visual or auditory event after a brief delay (e.g., Werner & Siqueland, 1978) and even also after a twenty-four-hour delay (e.g., Swain et al., 1993).

Research by Rovee-Collier (1995) has used a conditioned learning method in which infants learn a paired (or conjugate) relation between an object (a mobile over the crib) and their own actions (kicking). In the learning phase, a ribbon connects the infant's ankle to the mobile and when the infant moves the leg, the mobile moves. Memory for this learned relation increases linearly from 3 to 8 months of age. Babies aged 3 months can reproduce the learned actions seven days after initial learning and 6-month-olds can reproduce it fourteen days later (Rovee-Collier & Cuevas, 2009). This learning is context-dependent, especially for younger infants; changes from the learning to test condition in the color or pattern of the crib lining reduced memory performance (Rovee-Collier & Shyi, 1992). Reminders also matter. When infants get a reminder twenty-four hours before the test (see the mobile bobbing up and down), the duration of the memory increases; however, the length of delay between initial learning and the reminder affects retention (Galluccio & Rovee-Collier, 2007). Infants 3 months of age reminded immediately after learning remembered one day longer than average, infants reminded three days after learning remembered for an additional five days, and infants reminded five days after learning remembered for an additional sixteen days. A temporal limit on the utility of the reminder, which Rovee-Collier (1995) called a "time window," is important for learning. Infants are surrounded by a multitude of information and their attentional system is very responsive to it. Stimuli that are repeated are more important to learn than a stimulus encountered only once, and reminders likely strengthen and consolidate the memory (Hudson & Grysman, 2014). Without the ability to consolidate memories, the knowledge base would be a collection of disjointed information.

Studies that use deferred imitation indicate that infants are forming long-term memories late in the first year (Bauer, 2002). In these studies, the infant watches a model demonstrate an action sequence and later the infant is asked to reproduce it (e.g., assembling and striking a small gong). Nine-month-olds can remember a two-step action for about 1 month after first seeing it performed (Carver & Bauer, 1999). Both the number of action steps remembered and the length of delay between seeing an action and being able to reproduce it increase over the next year (see Lukowski & Bauer, 2014, for a review). Moreover, these memories can last a long time: 13-month-olds are able to remember a simple sequence (e.g., putting teddy bear to bed) after an eight-month-delay (Bauer, 2002).

### 5.1.2 Basic Memory Capacities

Basic memory capacities include the amount of information that can be held in STWM, or memory span, and the efficiency and speed of memory processing. These capacities change with development.

Memory span is usually tested by asking participants to repeat back in exact order a list of items previously told to them. Memory span for a series of numbers is about two units for 2-year-olds, four units for 5-year-olds, and seven units for older children and adults (Dempster, 1981). The reason for this developmental change is unknown and may reflect changes in STWM capacity or the development of other cognitive skills (Haden et al., 2011; Reznick, 2014). Improved language skills enable children to repeat the items in a list (verbally or mentally) more quickly (Hitch & Towse, 1995). Increased use of memory strategies, such as chunking, may be especially useful (Schneider, 2015). Chunking involves grouping information into smaller, more easily remembered sets based on a category (Chi, 1976). For example, a string of twelve digits, such as 1 7 7 6 1 8 1 2 1 9 4 1, is difficult to remember, but adults in the United States might chunk the numbers into more easily remembered groups (1776, 1812, and 1941 are national historical dates). Developmental changes occur because the categories used in chunking come from expansion of the general knowledge base.

Processing speed is how long it takes an individual to carry out a mental act, such as recognizing a stimulus or reading a word. Speed of processing increases with development on a range of tasks including reading comprehension, mental addition, retrieving names from memory, and visual search (Kail, 2000; Kail & Ferrer, 2007). Cross-cultural research suggests that practice plays a role. A study with 4- to 11-year-old children from China, Korea, and the United States found comparable performances in the youngest children, but processing speed for the older children developed more rapidly in Chinese than US children (Kail et al., 2013). Although the underlying mechanism is unknown, the researchers pointed out that the results coincide with previous findings that learning to read the complex orthography of the Chinese language leads to better visuospatial skill in Chinese children, which may boost processing speed (McBride-Chang et al., 2011).

Processing speed is related to processing efficiency because the more efficient a process is, the quicker it is. Over development, some memory processing becomes automatic and requires less attention from STWM. Biological changes, including increased efficiency in neural connections with myelination, may also play a role (Chevalier et al., 2015).

### 5.1.3 Strategic Memory

Strategies are deliberate techniques used to improve cognitive performance. A memory or mnemonic strategy helps a person retain and retrieve information more effectively and efficiently (Bjorklund et al., 2009). Children's use of three common mnemonics, rehearsal, organization, and elaboration, improves between 5 and 10 years of age. These developments play an important role in learning in school (Schneider, 2014).

Rehearsal involves repeating the information to be remembered either mentally or vocally. An early study found that children's spontaneous use of rehearsal increases with development (Flavell et al., 1966). Five- to eleven-year-old children were shown several pictures and told they would be asked about them later. Very few of the 5 and 6 year olds rehearsed the information, whereas 60 percent of the 7 and 8 year olds and over 85 percent of the 10 and 11 year olds did. Young children tend not to rehearse unless told to do so, and when they do rehearse they are less efficient than older children. For example, younger children will repeat the items to remember only once or twice even when more repetitions are needed (Naus, 1982). Rehearsal strategies also change in sophistication: Younger children usually rehearse each item singly, whereas older children use a cumulative strategy with each new item rehearsed along with previous items (Ornstein et al., 1975).

Children's use of organization also increases with development (Schneider, 2015). This strategy involves putting the items to be remembered together using categories or hierarchical relations. Children as young as 2 or 3 years old will use basic category labels to help them remember items (Waxman et al., 1991). Although 6- and 7-year-olds can organize items in groups to remember them, they often need to be reminded to do so (Ackerman, 1996). This behavior is called a production deficiency because children have the cognitive ability to use the strategy, but they lack knowledge of when and how to use it productively (Flavell, 1970). Children may use an appropriate strategy spontaneously, but not profit from using it. This so-called utilization deficiency is illustrated in a study in which 9- and 10-year-old children were trained to sort listed items into categories to aid memory (Bjorklund et al., 1994). When tested later, the children's memory for the items decreased even though they used the strategy.

By 10 to 12 years of age, most children use organizational strategies, such as categorizing, spontaneously and effectively to aid memory (Bjorklund et al., 2009).

The strategy of elaboration involves adding information to make the material more meaningful and, thus, easier to remember. Although adding information seems like it would increase the memory burden, this strategy is useful because we are more likely to remember something that is meaningful to us (Kee, 1994). The earlier example of chunking in expanding memory span illustrates this strategy. Children's use of elaboration is tested on tasks involving noun pairs (e.g., cat, apple; Pressley & Hilden, 2006). After studying the different pairs, the child is shown one of the items and asked to name the other item in the pair. An elaboration strategy would involve creating a connection between the items visually or verbally (e.g., a cat rolling an apple). This strategy is effective; however, children do not use it spontaneously until around 11 to 12 years of age.

World knowledge also aids memory, as illustrated in Chi's (1978) research with child chess experts, 8 to 13 years of age, and adult chess novices regarding their recall of a set of numbers and of chess positions. Although the children could not remember as many numbers as the adults, they surpassed the adults in memory for chess positions. The results demonstrate how experience in a domain can enhance memory for information in that domain but does not influence memory in other domains.

Social experience contributes to the development and use of memory strategies. Interactions with adults give children exposure to and practice with new strategies (Gauvain, 2001). For instance, adults help children understand how strategies can overcome capacity limitations of memory by encouraging children to put items into categories. When children have difficulty knowing which strategy to use (production deficiency) or in executing a strategy (utilization deficiency), adults can help children solve the immediate problem and provide tips that may be useful in the future.

Culture also contributes to strategic memory development (Mistry et al., 2013). Learning to use symbolic systems (e.g., language, numerals) and material tools (e.g., navigational aids, computers) can affect how memory is organized and retained (Maynard et al., 2005). When a child learns to write and then records information on paper to remember it later, the child is using a cultural tool, literacy, to store and retain this knowledge. There are other less obvious cultural contributions to memory development. Recall the earlier example of how learning the orthography of the Chinese language is related to memory span in Chinese children (McBride-Chang et al., 2011). Other research reports similar findings. One study compared the memory span of Lao and US American children on various tasks and found differences in visual and cross-modal tasks that favored the Lao children (Conant et al., 2003). The results were explained by associations between the tasks and literacy training in the Lao language, which alters the presentation of vowels and consonants to modify sounds and, consequently, emphasizes visuospatial processing more than English literacy does.

Cultures differ in the type of memory strategies they teach children. In societies that emphasize formal schooling, children need to learn large amounts of information at school, and rehearsal, organization, and elaboration strategies are especially useful. Strategies that rely on spatial thinking and oral traditions are more common in other societies and these strategies are passed on to children and influence memory development. In research comparing the spatial memory of Australian Aboriginal children reared in the desert and European Australian children reared in the city, Aboriginal children showed extensive and superior use of spatial memory strategies compared to children of European ancestry, whose memory relied more on naming the information as a list (Kearins, 1981). The Aboriginal children's success on these problems suggests the importance of spatial knowledge in way-finding in the vast desert occupied by the Aboriginal populations, as well as contemporary informal instructional practices in these indigenous communities that emphasize spatial thinking (Butterworth et al., 2011).

Note that both cultural and social experiences are involved when children learn about memory and how to use it. The conventions and traditions for organizing and storing knowledge in a culture are passed onto children socially by more experienced cultural members.

### 5.1.4 Autobiographical Memory

Episodic memory consists of information about events, and much of it is autobiographical and includes personal experiences in an individual's life (Bauer, 2006). Autobiographical memories serve many developmental functions. They help to define a child's identity and sense of self, and they are conversational tools that help children develop and maintain relationships (Howe, 2015).

Children first refer to past events at about 18 months, often about recently completed actions or well-learned routines (Howe, 2014). At 20 months of age, children begin to refer to events in the more distant past, and by age 2, they remember everyday routines or scripts (e.g., going to a restaurant; Bauer & Fivush, 2010; Howe et al., 2003). When children talk about scripts, they often include information about the child's role in a routine situation, reflecting the integration of semantic and episodic aspects of autobiographical memory (Howe, 2015).

Autobiographical memory is linked to children's social experiences. During family interaction, discussion of past events occurs about five to seven times an hour (Fivush et al., 1996). Parents talk directly to children about the past, and they talk to others about the past in the child's presence (Haden & Ornstein, 2009). When children are around 2½ years of age, parents assume most of the responsibility for conversations about shared memories (Hudson, 1990). By age 3, children's contributions increase (Fivush & Hamond, 1989). During shared remembering, children learn about what to remember and how to formulate their memories (Bauer, 2006). These conversations may also help children cope with difficult or emotional experiences such as a hurricane or asthma attack (Fivush & Sales, 2004).

Much of conversation about autobiographical memories adopts a narrative form, an account of an event that is temporally sequenced (Engel, 1995). Children's narratives describe the aspects of the event that were important and understandable to them. Although they are usually brief, young children's narratives may have deep meaning for a child because of their personal significance (Engel & Li, 2004). Other people help shape the memory by noting what aspects are interesting or important to remember. When adults show interest in a memory, it may increase the likelihood of it being retold, which will strengthen the memory (Haden et al., 2001). Reactions by others may even become part of the memory.

The ways that mothers engage in joint reminiscing with young children relate to the quality and duration of children's autobiographical memories (Fivush, 2014). When mothers use an elaborative style, which involves asking open-ended questions about and elaborating on a memory, children remember more detailed information about the event than when mothers use a pragmatic style, which relies mainly on closed-ended questions about facts (Howe et al., 2003). Reminiscing style is not a stable trait of mothers, however. Mothers can be trained to use a more elaborative style and when they do, it is related positively to children's immediate and 6-month memory recall (Van Bergen et al., 2009).

Shared reminiscence is culturally widespread and helps to communicate family and cultural values to children (Nelson, 2014). In one study, children between 3 and 8 years of age from China and the United States were asked to recount four autobiographical events (Wang, 2004). Memories of the US American children included much personal detail, especially about the child's own experiences and feelings. Memories of the Chinese children concentrated on social aspects of their lives (e.g., social relationships, routines involving others). These patterns are consistent with the different emphases on autonomy and social connections in the two cultures.

Not all members of a culture behave in exactly the same way when they interact with children about autobiographical memories. One study examined the use of elaboration during joint reminiscing by middle-class mothers and their 4-year-old children in Berlin, Stockholm, and Tallinn, Estonia (Tõugu et al., 2012). All three cultures value autonomy (independence, personal uniqueness) over relatedness (interdependence, social relationships). Within these culture groups, there were different patterns and rates in mothers' use of open-ended questions, statements, and verbal confirmations – all aspects of an elaborative reminiscing style. Similar variation has been found within US samples (Fivush, 2014).

## 5.2 Metacognition and Executive Function

Between early and middle childhood, children's abilities to understand thinking, or metacognition, and to control their own thoughts and actions, or executive function, improve considerably with profound consequences. Although these capacities begin early in childhood, they are prominent between 4 and 7 years of age.

Both metacognition and executive function are domain-general capacities that result from developments in self-reflection, the capacity to recognize and evaluate one's ongoing thoughts and actions and, if needed, adjust behaviors during an ongoing activity (Lyons & Zelazo, 2011). The development of metacognition and executive function corresponds with changes in the frontal cortex that begin in early childhood (Diamond, 2011).

### 5.2.1 Metacognition

Metacognition is knowledge about cognition. It includes awareness of cognitive activity and the ability to reflect on and evaluate knowledge (Lyons & Ghetti, 2010). For instance, 4-year-olds know that it is harder to remember a long list of items than a short list, that a person's characteristics (e.g., clothing) do not influence memory performance, and that you need to put in more effort on a hard than an easy task. Between 5 and 7 years of age, these abilities continue to develop and enable children to plan and carry out complex tasks (Friedman et al., 2014; McCormack & Atance, 2011). Children will appraise in advance how much effort is needed to do an activity, determine which cognitive abilities would be useful, and regulate their effort as the activity is carried out – all of which reflect metacognition (Niebaum & Munakata, 2020).

Metacognition is critical for solving many types of problems, and it is important for academic success as children advance in school (Zelazo et al., 2016). To do well in school, it is important to attend to and follow instructions. With development, children pay closer attention when instructions are given, ask questions if instructions are unclear, and remember and follow instructions carefully during an activity. There is also increasing sensitivity to how external support can aid cognitive activity as well as improvements in determining the value of external information, such as reminders and hints (Redshaw et al., 2018; Selmeczy & Ghetti, 2019).

Given the importance of metacognition to academic performance, research has focused on how teachers can help children implement these skills during lessons (Ornstein & Coffman, 2020). A longitudinal study helped teachers increase their use of cognitive processing language in class instruction, such as asking children "What are some of the strategies you could use to figure the answer out?" The researchers found improvements in children's use of strategies, such as organization, following the intervention, especially among children with lower levels of self-regulatory learning skills.

Further study of the role of metacognition in early to middle childhood, especially in the school context, is needed. However, one difficulty in studying metacognition is that it often relies on interviewing children, and children may have these skills before they can verbalize much about them (Simons et al., 2020).

### 5.2.2 Executive Function

Children's ability to consciously control their thoughts and actions improves with development. A set of cognitive capacities underlies these changes, collectively referred to as executive function (Müller & Kerns, 2015). These capacities include the ability to regulate attention, hold information in working memory, inhibit impulsive responses, and flexibly shift one's mental frame during goal-directed activity.

As children acquire more conscious control of their thoughts and actions, their self-regulatory ability improves substantially (Best et al., 2009). This ability is important to mature cognitive and socioemotional functioning and for carrying out goal-directed activities (Carlson, 2003; Rothbart et al., 2011). Self-regulatory skills let children inhibit impulsive responses and, instead, use higher cognitive functions to understand an ongoing activity and manage their behavior to reach the goal. The neurological basis of this development involves changes in the frontal cortex and neural connections that interpret and regulate responses to incoming information (Zelazo et al., 2010). Impairments in this area are associated with learning disorders related to executive function (Johnson & de Haan, 2015).

Executive function skills are especially important for learning in academic contexts (Best et al., 2011; Roebers, 2017). Academic success relies, in part, on children's ability to regulate their behavior to expectations in the classroom (Blair, 2002). By the time children begin school, they are expected to stay focused on a task, ignore irrelevant information, plan an activity, and monitor progress in reaching the goal as the activity progresses. All are executive function skills. Kindergarten teachers value self-regulation skills above academic skills as an index of school readiness (Blair & Diamond, 2008). Other executive function skills are also important. Children acquire understanding of their own and others' cognitive abilities, which gives them insight into learning more generally, for example, 7-year-olds know it is easier to relearn information they have forgotten than learn it for the first time.

Social experience contributes to the development of executive function, including parent–child interaction in the form of scaffolding and through warm and sensitive caregiving (Bernier et al., 2012; Hammond et al., 2012). Adverse family environments, such as disorganization, unpredictability, and lack of warmth and support can impede this development (Blair, 2010). Relationships with peers are also important (Gauvain, 2016). Children with poorer executive function skills have more problems with peers (Holmes et al., 2016). Explicit training in developing executive function, such as computer-based activities (see Diamond, 2012) and mindfulness training (Schonert-Reichl et al., 2015), indicate that this development is malleable and responsive to intervention.

## 5.3 Problem-Solving and Reasoning

The ability to solve problems is vital to everyday functioning. Problem-solving entails identifying a goal, determining the steps to reach the goal, executing those steps, and monitoring progress toward reaching the goal (Munakata, 2006). Usually, one or more obstacles interfere with reaching the goal and need to be overcome.

Problem-solving integrates many cognitive capabilities – attention, perception, memory, and symbolic systems, including language. Some problems require reasoning, a type of thinking that goes beyond the information in a specific problem by making inferences about the nature of the problem and whether there are any rules or standards that may be applied (Ricco, 2015). For example, when solving a problem in elementary physics, such as how to balance objects on a balance beam, a person may have the insight, or infer, rules that govern balance.

Because of the complex nature of problem-solving, this skill develops over a long period of time (Garton, 2004). Rudimentary skill at solving problems is present in infancy; for example, 8-month-olds will deliberately grab a cloth to pull it closer to play with the toy resting on it (Willatts, 1990). Competence at solving complex problems continues to develop through adolescence and into early adulthood (Gauvain & Reynolds, 2011).

### 5.3.1 The Contextual Nature of Problem-Solving

Effective problem-solving depends on the way a person understands or encodes the problem to work on it mentally. With development, children allocate their attention more effectively, encode more features of a problem, and are better at updating problem information and evaluating progress in reaching the goal (Kaller et al., 2008). Children also use more strategies, conscious cognitive or behavioral activities that enhance problem-solving (Pressley & Hilden, 2006; Schneider, 2010). Increased use of strategies, such as generating, using, and ignoring evidence, enhances children's problem-solving, especially in scientific thinking (Klahr, 2000). The ability to choose a more effective strategy when alternative strategies are available also improves (Siegler & Chen, 2002).

Sociocultural experience contributes to the development of problem-solving. Children learn much about solving problems from people with whom they have regular contact (Gauvain et al., 2018). Culture affects the types of problems people solve, the manner in which they solve them, and the tools and resources used in these efforts (Goodnow, 1990). When and how people solve problems is often organized around cultural values, such as cooperation or efficiency. Among European Americans, competition and speed of performance influence how children solve problems, whereas in many African cultures social responsibility is a preeminent influence (Serpell, 2011). Solving problems often involves cultural tools, both symbolic (e.g., literacy, numerals) and material (e.g., computer technology), and over development children learn to use these tools to solve problems.

The development of problem-solving and reasoning has consequences for academic success especially as children advance in school and tackle more difficult subject matter (National Academies of Sciences, Engineering, and Medicine, 2018, 2021; Wentzel & Ramani, 2016). These skills also impact children's lives outside of school. Many of the challenges children face, such as how to manage their time, meet responsibilities, get along with others, and deal with positive and negative experiences, require problem-solving and reasoning. Psychologists who help children at risk for personal, social, and emotional difficulties often concentrate on the development of these skills (Bierman et al., 2019).

### 5.3.2 Developing Skill at Solving Different Types of Problems

The following paragraphs describe children's developing skills in solving problems involving rules, analogies, and deduction. Children's developing use of cognitive tools to solve problems is also described.

With development, children increasingly seek systematic information or rules about how elements of a problem relate to and affect one another. This development is illustrated in research in which children learned the rules of balance by placing weights on a balance beam, a board resting on a fulcrum (Siegler, 1991). Children 3 years of age did not use rules to solve this problem; 4- to 5-year-olds used a simple rule (if weights on both sides are equal, the side whose weights are farther from the fulcrum is heavier), 9-year-olds used a rule that combined weight and distance, and 13-year-olds used a rule based on torque (a measure of the effectiveness of a force). Thus, as children develop, they consider more dimensions of the problem and discern rules that accommodate them. This development has implications regarding children's scientific reasoning and the design of science education (Klahr et al., 2011).

Reasoning using analogies involves the inference that if two or more objects or situations resemble each other in some respects they are likely to resemble each other in other respects (Richland et al., 2006). Young children have difficulty with analogies presented in the form of A:B as C:? (e.g., "foot is to leg as hand is to what?"). However, when simpler relations are used, such as perceptual similarity, young children are able to use analogies to solve a problem. In one study, pictures of familiar items were presented as (A) Chocolate: (B) Melted chocolate as (C) Snowman: (D) Which picture? (Goswami & Brown, 1990). Five picture choices were shown and one was of a melted snowman, which is the correct response. Three-year-old children were correct 52 percent of the time, 4-year-olds were correct 89 percent of the time, and 5-year-olds were correct 99 percent of the time. This finding has implications for learning subjects like mathematics that require the application of abstract principles across similar problems (Richland et al., 2007).

Deductive reasoning is a form of reasoning based on a set of premises or stated propositions. A syllogism requires deductive reasoning because it includes a major premise, a minor premise, and a conclusion; for example: All virtues are good; Kindness is a virtue; Therefore, kindness is good. Hawkins and colleagues (1984) presented simple versions of this type of problem to 4- and 5-year-old children, such as: Pogs wear blue boots; Tom is a pog; Does Tom wear blue boots? The children did well on these syllogisms, suggesting that a basic understanding of deductive reasoning is present at this age. A related form of reasoning regarding items in an ordered sequence is called transitive inference, for example, inferring that Jane is taller than Kim when told that "Jane is taller than Emily and Emily is taller than Kim" (Ricco, 2015). Children younger than 6 or 7 years of age have difficulty with this type of problem, however, when information is presented in a familiar form, for example when asked to arrange Mama, Papa, and Baby Bear in the Goldilocks story in order of size, even 4-year-old children do well (Goswami, 1995).

Many symbolic (e.g., literacy, numerals) and material (e.g., computer technology, maps) resources, or cognitive tools, are used to aid problem-solving and their use changes with development. Children's understanding and use of scale models and pictures to solve problems change between 2 and 3 years of age. Three-year-olds, but not 2.5-year-olds, can use a scale model of a room as a source of information about the actual room (e.g., finding an object in the actual room after seeing a similar toy object hidden in the model room). This shift reflects the understanding that objects can have dual representation, that is, an object can have an identity in itself and also represent something else (DeLoache, 2004).

One common activity that involves cognitive tools is learning about and using large-scale space (Liben & Christensen, 2011). Cognitive tools that support spatial thinking include directions and maps, and understanding and using these tools improve over childhood (Liben & Downs, 2015). Young children, 4 to 5 years of age, have a basic understanding of what maps represent (e.g., show locations) and how they can be used (e.g., to find a place), although they do not understand many of the symbolic representations (e.g., they expect a road shown as red on a map to be red; Liben, 2009).

Cultural tools used to communicate about and travel in space have changed significantly with computerized navigational aids such as geographic information systems (GIS) and global positioning systems (GPS; Downs, 2014). Real-time navigational information in handheld computers helps people plan routes that can be updated with current travel conditions. Even people living in geographically isolated regions of the world use these tools to carry out daily activities, such as finding clean water for household use and livestock (Mpogole et al., 2008). These new technologies are also influencing geography instruction in K-12 classrooms (Collins, 2018). Questions have been raised about how widespread use of geospatial technologies will affect children's understanding of space and reliance on external devices for solving spatial problems (Gauvain, 2014). The impact on culture will also be important to understand, as seen in the Sami community, a reindeer-herding culture in northern Scandinavia whose lifestyle involves much long-distance travel. The Sami now use mapping technology to explore and teach their children about the environment (Cogos et al., 2017). Indigenous place names and journeys are not represented in these tools, instead they use Western conceptions of spatial navigation and names of the region. As the Sami people adopt this cognitive tool, they are concerned about the loss of cultural identity in the younger generation.

## 6 Conclusion

Over the first decade of life, cognitive functioning changes greatly as children come to understand and engage with the world. The way that cognition develops was shaped by human evolutionary history, a history in which social life and culture evolved in step with human biology. Children are born with a brain and neural system that are tuned to the people around them, who, in turn, care for children and provide the foundation for cognitive growth. The pace and pattern of cognitive development reflect several key features of the human species: the immaturity of the brain at birth, the flexibility or plasticity of the brain in response to experience, a protracted developmental course, the propensity to form strong social and emotional ties, and a lifestyle rooted in an organized social group – culture – that maintains and passes its valued practices, tools, and behaviors across generations.

This Element describes the main theories of cognitive development along with research discoveries in several important cognitive abilities: attention, language, social cognition, memory, metacognition and executive function, and problem-solving and reasoning. Biological and social contributions were considered side by side, and cultural contributions were highlighted. As children participate in social interactions and learn to use cultural symbols and tools to organize and support their thinking, the behaviors and understandings of the social community and the culture more broadly become an integral part of children's thoughts and actions. Without the capacity to learn socially, human cognition would be markedly different from what it is today.

Appreciating cognitive development as a biological, psychological, social, and cultural process introduces many new questions and topics to this field of study. Future research will benefit from theoretical framing that includes detailed accounts of how cognitive development emerges in various social and cultural settings. It will also be important to examine cognitive development during cultural change. The ecology of childhood is changing rapidly around the world. Increased urbanization, massive shifts in the economic, political, social, and environmental conditions of life, along with changes in the communicative environment have significant impact on children's lives. To understand cognitive development during cultural change, it will be necessary to study how children spend their time on a regular basis – the activities they do, with whom they do activities, and the tools and resources that support their activities. This research must be guided by theory that recognizes how sociocultural experience together with children's own actions contribute to the development of thinking and cognitive skills.

# References

Ackerman, B. P. (1996). Induction of a memory retrieval strategy by young children. *Journal of Experimental Child Psychology*, *62*, 243–271. https://doi.org/10.1006/jecp.1996.0030

Adamson, L. B., & Bakeman, R. (1991). The development of shared attention during infancy. In R. Vasta (Ed.), *Annals of child development* (Vol. 8, pp. 1–41). London: Kingsley.

Akhtar, N., Dunham, F., & Dunham, P. (1991). Directive interactions and early vocabulary development: The role of joint attentional focus. *Journal of Child Language*, *18*, 41–49. https://doi.org/10.1017/S0305000900013283

Akhtar, N., Tolins, J., & Fox Tree, J. E. (2019). Young children's word learning through overhearing: Next steps. In J. S. Horst & J. von Koss Torkildsen (Eds.), *International handbook of language acquisition* (pp. 427–441). New York: Taylor & Francis Group.

Amso, D., & Scerif, G. (2015). The attentive brain: Insights from developmental cognitive neuroscience. *Nature Reviews Neuroscience*, *16*, 606–619. https://doi.org/10.1038/nrn4025

Arterberry, M. E., & Bornstein, M. H. (2001). Three-month-old infants' categorization of animals and vehicles based on static and dynamic attributes. *Journal of Experimental Child Psychology*, *80*, 333–346. https://doi.org/10.1006/jecp.2001.2637

Aslin, R. N., & Newport, E. L. (2012). Statistical learning: From acquiring specific items to forming general rules. *Current Directions in Psychological Science*, *21*, 170–176. https://doi.org/10.1177/0963721412436806

Atkinson, R. C., & Shiffrin, R. M. (1968). Human memory: A proposed system and its control processes. In K. W. Spence & J. Spence (Eds.), *Advances in the psychology of learning and motivation: Research and theory* (Vol. 2, pp. 89–195). New York: Academic Press.

Austin, K., Theakston, A., Lieven, E., & Tomasello, M. (2014). Young children's understanding of denial. *Developmental Psychology*, *50*, 2061–2070. https://psycnet.apa.org/doi/10.1037/a0037179

Baillargeon, R., Scott, R., & Bian, L. (2016). Psychological reasoning in infancy. *Annual Review of Psychology*, *67*, 159–186. https://doi.org/10.1146/annurev-psych-010213-115033

Bakeman, R., Adamson, L. B., Konner, M., & Barr, R. G. (1990).Kung infancy: The social context of object exploration. *Child Development*, *61*, 794–809. https://doi.org/10.2307/1130964

Baldwin, D. A. (1991). Infants' contribution to the achievement of joint reference. *Child Development, 62*, 875–890. https://doi.org/10.2307/1131140

Baltes, P. B. (2006). *Lifespan development and the brain*. Cambridge: Cambridge University Press.

Bandura, A. (1989). Social cognitive theory. In R. Vasta (Ed.), *Annals of child development: Six theories of child development* (Vol. 6, pp. 1–60). Greenwich, CT: JAI Press.

Bandura, A. (1997). *Self-efficacy: The exercise of control*. New York: Freeman.

Bates, E., & Elman, J. (1996). Learning rediscovered. *Science, 274*, 1849–1850. https://doi.org/10.1126/science.274.5294.1849

Bauer, P. J. (2002). Long-term recall memory: Behavioral and neuro-developmental changes in the first 2 years of life. *Current Directions in Psychological Science, 11*, 137–141. https://doi.org/10.1111/1467-8721.00186

Bauer, P. J. (2006). Constructing a past in infancy: A neuro-developmental account. *Trends in Cognitive Sciences, 10*, 175–181. https://doi.org/10.1016/j.tics.2006.02.009

Bauer, P. J., & Fivush, R. (2010). Context and consequences of autobiographical memory development. *Cognitive Development, 25*, 303–308. https://doi.org/10.1016/j.cogdev.2010.08.001

Bernier, A., Carlson, S. M., Deschênes, M., & Matte-Gagné, C. (2012). Social factors in the development of early executive functioning: A closer look at the caregiving environment. *Developmental Science, 15*, 12–24. https://doi.org/10.1111/j.1467-7687.2011.01093.x

Best, J. R., Miller, P. H., & Jones, L. L. (2009). Executive functions after age 5: Changes and correlates. *Developmental Review, 29*, 180–200. https://doi.org/10.1016/j.dr.2009.05.002

Best, J. R., Miller, P. H., & Naglieri, J. A. (2011). Relations between executive function and academic achievement from ages 5 to 17 in a large, representative national sample. *Learning and Individual Differences, 21*(4), 327–336. https://doi.org/10.1016/j.lindif.2011.01.007

Bialystok, E. (2015). Bilingualism and the development of executive function: The role of attention. *Child Development Perspectives, 9*, 117–121. https://doi.org/10.1111/cdep.12116

Bierman, K. L., Coie, J. D., Dodge, K. A. et al. (2019). *The fast track program for children at risk: Preventing antisocial behavior*. New York: Guilford.

Bjorklund, D. F. (2020). *Cambridge elements child development: Child development in evolutionary perspective*. Cambridge: Cambridge University Press.

Bjorklund, D. F., & Causey, K. B. (2018). *Children's thinking: Cognitive development and individual differences* (6th ed.). Los Angeles, CA: Sage.

Bjorklund, D. F., Dukes, C., & Brown, R. D. (2009). The development of memory strategies. In M. L. Courage & N. Cowan (Eds.), *The development of memory in infancy and childhood* (pp. 145–175). New York: Psychology Press.

Bjorklund, D. F., Schneider, W., Cassel, W. S., & Ashley, E. (1994). Training and extension of a memory strategy: Evidence for utilization deficiencies in the acquisition of an organizational strategy in high- and low-IQ children. *Child Development, 65*, 951–965. https://doi.org/10.2307/1131430

Blair, C. (2002). School readiness: Integrating cognition and emotion in a neurobiological conceptualization of children's functioning at school entry. *American Psychologist, 57*, 111–127. https://doi.org/10.1037/0003-066X.57.2.111

Blair, C. (2010). Stress and the development of self-regulation in context. *Child Development Perspectives, 4*, 181–188. https://doi.org/10.1111/j.1750-8606 .2010.00145.x

Blair, C., & Diamond, A. (2008). Biological processes in prevention and intervention: The promotion of self-regulation as a means of preventing school failure. *Developmental Psychopathology, 20*, 899–911. https://psycnet.apa.org/ doi/10.1017/S0954579408000436

Bornstein, M. H. (1995). Form and function: Implications for studies of culture and human development. *Culture & Psychology, 1*, 123–137. https://doi.org/ 10.1177/1354067x9511009

Bornstein, M. H. (2009). Toward a model of culture↔parent↔child transactions. In A. Sameroff (Ed.), *The transactional model of development: How children and contexts shape each other* (pp. 139–161). Washington, DC: American Psychological Association. https://psycnet.apa.org/doi/10.1037/ 11877-000

Bornstein, M. H. (2015). Emergence and early development of color vision and color perception. In A. Elliot, M. Fairchild, & A. Franklin (Eds.), *Handbook of color psychology* (pp. 149–179). New York: Cambridge University Press. https://doi.org/10.1017/CBO9781107337930

Bornstein, M. H. (2021). The SARS-CoV-2 pandemic: Issues for families, parents, and children. In M. H. Bornstein (Ed.), *Psychological insights for understanding COVID-19 and families, parents, and children* (pp. 1–69). London: Routledge.

Bornstein, M. H., Cote, L. R., Maital, S. et al. (2004). Cross-linguistic analysis of vocabulary in young children: Spanish, Dutch, French, Hebrew, Italian,

Korean, and American English. *Child Development, 75,* 1115–1139. https://doi.org/10.1111/j.1467-8624.2004.00729.x

Bornstein, M. H., Putnick, D. L., Cote, L. R., Haynes, O. M. H., & Suwalsky, J. T. D. (2015). Mother-infant contingent vocalizations in 11 countries. *Psychological Science, 26,* 1272–1284. https://doi.org/10.1177/0956797615586796

Bornstein, M. H., Tal, J., & Tamis-LeMonda, C. (1991). Parenting in cross-cultural perspective. In M. H. Bornstein (Ed.), *Cultural approaches to parenting* (pp. 69–90). Hillsdale, NJ: Erlbaum.

Bowlby, J. (1988). *A secure base: Parent-child attachment and healthy human development.* New York: Basic Books.

Bronfenbrenner, U., & Morris, P. A. (2006). The bioecological model of human development. In R. M. Lerner (Ed.), *Handbook of child psychology: Theoretical models of human development* (6th ed., Vol. 1, pp. 793–828). Hoboken, NJ: Wiley.

Brooks, R., & Meltzoff, A. N. (2014). Gaze following: A mechanism for building social connections between infants and adults. In M. Mikulincer & P. R. Shaver (Eds.), *Mechanisms of social connection: From brain to group* (pp. 167–183). Washington, DC: American Psychological Association.

Brosseau-Liard, P. E., & Birch, S. A. J. (2011). Epistemic states and traits: Preschoolers appreciate the differential informativeness of situation-specific and person-specific cues to knowledge. *Child Development, 82,* 1788–1796. https://doi.org/10.1111/j.1467-8624.2011.01662.x

Brown, P., & Gaskins, S. (2014). Language acquisition and language socialization. In N. J. Enfield, P. Kockelman, & J. Sidnell (Eds.), *The Cambridge handbook of linguistic anthropology* (pp. 187–226). New York: Cambridge University Press. https://doi.org/10.1017/CBO9781139342872.010

Brownell, C. A., & Carriger, M. S. (1990). Changes in cooperation and self-other differentiation during the second year. *Child Development, 61,* 1164–1174. https://doi.org/10.2307/1130884

Brownell, C. A., Ramani, G. B., & Zerwas, S. (2006). Becoming a social partner with peers: Cooperation and social understanding in one- and two-year-olds. *Child Development, 77,* 803–821. https://doi.org/10.1111/j.1467-8624.2006.00904.x

Bruner, J. S., & Sherwood, V. (1976). Early rule structure: The case of "peek-aboo." In R. Harre (Ed.), *Life sentences* (pp. 55–62). London: Wiley.

Budwig, N. (1990). The linguistic marking of nonprototypical agency: An exploration into children's use of passives. *Linguistics, 28,* 1121–1252. https://doi.org/10.1515/ling.1990.28.6.1221

Burdelski, M. (2010). Socializing politeness routines: Action, other-orientation, and embodiment in a Japanese preschool. *Journal of Pragmatics*, *42*, 1606–1621. https://doi.org/10.1016/j.pragma.2009.11.007

Butler, L. P., Ronfard, S., & Corriveau, K. H. (2020). *The questioning child: Insights from psychology and education*. New York: Cambridge University Press.

Butterworth, B., Reeve, R., & Reynolds, F. (2011). Using mental representations of space when words are unavailable: Studies of enumeration and arithmetic in indigenous Australia. *Journal of Cross-Cultural Psychology*, *42*, 630–638. https://doi.org/10.1177%2F0022022111406020

Butterworth, G. (1995). Origins of mind in perception and action. In C. Moore & P. J. Dunham (Eds.), *Joint attention: Its origins and its role in development* (pp. 29–40). Hillsdale, NJ: Erlbaum.

Callaghan, T., Moll, H., Rakoczy, H. et al. (2011). Early social cognition in three cultural contexts. *Monographs of the Society for Research in Child Development*, *76* (Serial No. 299), 1–142. https://doi.org/10.1111/j.1540-5834.2011.00603.x

Callaghan, T., Rochat, P., Lillard, A. et al. (2005). Synchrony in the onset of mental state reasoning: Evidence from five cultures. *Psychological Science*, *16*(5), 378–384. https://doi.org/10.1111%2Fj.0956-7976.2005.01544.x

Cameron-Faulkner, T., Malik, N., Steele, C. et al. (2021). A cross-cultural analysis of early prelinguistic gesture development and its relationship to language development. *Child Development*, *92*, 273–290. https://doi.org/10.1111/cdev.13406

Campbell, S. B. (2000). Developmental perspectives on attention deficit disorder. In A. Sameroff, M. Lewis, & S. Miller (Eds.), *Handbook of child psychopathology* (2nd ed., pp. 383–401). New York: Plenum Press.

Carey, S. (1978). The child as a word learner. In M. Halle, J. Bresnan, & G. Miller (Eds.), *Linguistic theory and psychological reality* (pp. 264–293). Cambridge, MA: MIT Press.

Carlson, S. M. (2003). Executive function in context: Development, measurement, theory, and experience. *Monographs of the Society for Research in Child Development*, *68* (Serial No. 274), 138–151. https://doi.org/10.1111/j.1540-5834.2003.06803012.x

Carpendale, J., & Lewis, C. (2021). *What makes us human: How minds develop through social interactions*. New York: Taylor & Francis Group.

Carpendale, J., Lewis, C., & Müller, U. (2018). *The development of children's thinking: Its social and communicative foundations*. Los Angeles, CA: Sage.

Carpenter, M., Akhtar, N., & Tomasello, M. (1998a). 14- through 18-month-old infants differentially imitate intentional and accidental actions. *Infant*

*Behavior and Development, 21*, 315–330. https://doi.org/10.1016/S0163-6383(98)90009-1

Carpenter, M., Nagell, K., & Tomasello, M. (1998b). Social cognition, joint attention, and communicative competence from 9 to 15 months of age. *Monographs of the Society for Research in Child Development, 63* (Serial No. 255), 1–143. https://psycnet.apa.org/doi/10.2307/1166214

Carver, L. J., & Bauer, P. J. (1999). When the event is more than the sum of its parts: 9-month-olds' long-term ordered recall. *Memory, 7*, 147–174. https://psycnet.apa.org/doi/10.1080/741944070

Chavajay, P., & Rogoff, B. (1999). Cultural variation in the management of attention by children and their caregivers. *Developmental Psychology, 35*, 1079–1090. https://psycnet.apa.org/doi/10.1037/0012-1649.35.4.1079

Chevalier, N., Kurth, S., Doucette, M. R. et al. (2015). Myelination is associated with processing speed in early childhood: Preliminary insights. *PLoS One, 10* (10), e0139897. https://doi.org/10.1371/journal.pone.0139897

Chi, M. T. H. (1976). Short term memory limitations in children: Capacity or processing deficits? *Memory and Cognition, 4*, 559–572. https://doi.org/10.3758/BF03213219

Chi, M. T. H. (1978). Knowledge structures and memory development. In R. S. Siegler (Ed.), *Children's thinking: What develops?* (pp. 73–96). Hillsdale, NJ: Erlbaum.

Chomsky, N. (1968). *Language and mind*. New York: Harcourt, Brace & World.

Cicchetti, D., & Rogosch, F. A. (1996). Equifinality and multifinality in developmental psychopathology. *Development and Psychopathology, 8*, 597–600. https://psycnet.apa.org/doi/10.1017/S0954579400007318

Clark, E. V. (2019). Research on first language acquisition: A brief history. In J. S. Horst & J. von Koss Torkildsen (Eds.), *International handbook of language acquisition* (pp. 3–19). New York: Taylor & Francis Group.

Cogos, S., Roue, M., & Roturier, S. (2017). Sami place names and maps: Transmitting knowledge of a cultural landscape in contemporary contexts. *Arctic, Antarctic, and Alpine Research, 49*, 43–51. https://doi.org/10.1657/AAAR0016-042

Cole, M. (1996). *Cultural psychology: A once and future discipline*. Cambridge, MA: Harvard University Press.

Collins, L. (2018). The impact of paper versus digital map technology on students' spatial thinking skill acquisition. *Journal of Geography, 117*, 137–152. https://doi.org/10.1080/00221341.2017.1374990

Colombo, J. (2001). The development of visual attention in infancy. *Annual Review of Psychology, 52*, 337–367. https://doi.org/10.1146/annurev.psych.52.1.337

Conant, L. L., Fastenau, P. S., Giordani, B. et al. (2003). Environmental influences on primary memory development: A cross-cultural study of memory span in Lao and American children. *Journal of Clinical and Experimental Neuropsychology*, *25*, 1102–1116. https://doi.org/10.1076/jcen.25.8.1102.16722

Conradt, E. (2017). Using principles of behavioral epigenetics to advance research on early-life stress. *Child Development Perspectives*, *11*, 107–112. https://doi.org/10.1111/cdep.12219

Cooper, R. P., & Aslin, R. N. (1990). Preference for infant-directed speech in the first month after birth. *Child Development*, *61*, 1584–1595. https://psycnet .apa.org/doi/10.2307/1130766

Corriveau, K., Harris, P. L., Meins, E. et al. (2009). Young children's trust in their mothers' claims: Longitudinal links with attachment security in infancy. *Child Development*, *80*, 750–761. https://psycnet.apa.org/doi/10.1017/ CBO9780511750946.005

Cowan, N. (2014). Short-term and working memory in childhood. In P. J. Bauer & R. Fivush (Eds.), *The Wiley handbook on the development of children's memory* (Vol. 1, pp. 202–230). Chichester: Wiley-Blackwell.

Cowan, N., AuBuchon, A. M., Gilchrist, A. L., Ricker, T. J., & Saults, J. S. (2011). Age differences in visual working memory capacity: Not based on encoding limitations. *Developmental Science*, *14*, 1066–1074. https://doi.org/ 10.1111/j.1467-7687.2011.01060.x

Cowell, J. M., Sommerville, J. A., & Decety, J. (2019). That's not fair: Children's neural computations of fairness and their impact on resource allocation behaviors and judgments. *Developmental Psychology*, *55*(11), 2299–2310. https://doi.org/10.1037/dev0000813

de Haan, M. (2008). Neurocognitive mechanisms for the development of face processing. In C. A. Nelson & M. Luciana (Eds.), *The handbook of developmental cognitive neuroscience* (2nd ed., pp. 509–520). Cambridge, MA: MIT Press.

De Houwer, A. (2021). *Bilingual development in childhood*. New York: Cambridge University Press.

DeLoache, J. S. (2004). Becoming symbol minded. *Trends in Cognitive Science*, *8*, 66–70. https://psycnet.apa.org/doi/10.1016/j.tics.2003.12.004

Dempster, F. N. (1981). Memory span: Sources of individual and developmental differences. *Psychological Bulletin*, *89*, 63–100. https://doi.org/10.1016/ 0022-0965(78)90122-4

Diamond, A. (2011). Biological and social influences on cognitive control processes dependent on the prefrontal cortex. In O. Braddick, J. Atkinson, & G. Innocenti (Eds.), *Progress in brain research* (Vol. 189, pp. 319–339). New York: Elsevier.

Diamond, A. (2012). Activities and programs that improve children's executive functions. *Current Directions in Psychological Science, 21,* 335–341. https://doi.org/10.1177%2F0963721412453722

Diaz, R. M. (1983). Thought and two languages: The impact of bilingualism on cognitive development. *Review of Research in Education, 10,* 23–54. https://doi.org/10.3102%2F0091732X010001023

Dick, A. S., Garcia, N. L., Pruden, S. M. et al. (2019). No evidence for a bilingual executive function advantage in the ABCD study. *Nature Human Behavior, 3,* 692–701. https://doi.org/10.1038/s41562-019-0609-3

Downs, R. M. (2014). Coming of age in the geospatial revolution: The geographic self re-defined. *Human Development, 57,* 35–57. https://doi.org/10.1159/000358319

Dunn, J. (2002). Emotional development in early childhood: A social relationship perspective. In R. Davidson, H. H. Goldsmith, & K. Scherer (Eds.), *The handbook of affective science* (pp. 332–346). Oxford: Oxford University Press.

Elman, J. L., Bates, E. A., Johnson, M. H. et al. (1996). *Rethinking innateness: A connectionist perspective on development.* Cambridge, MA: MIT Press.

Engel, S. (1995). *The stories children tell: Making sense of the narratives of childhood.* New York: Freeman.

Engel, S., & Li, A. (2004). Narratives, gossip, and shared experience: How and what young children know about the lives of others. In J. M. Lucariello, J. A. Hudson, R. Fivush, & P. J. Bauer (Eds.), *The development of the mediated mind: Sociocultural context and cognitive development* (pp. 151–174). Mahwah, NJ: Erlbaum.

Ervin-Tripp, S. (1996). Context in language. In D. I. Slobin, J. Gerhardt, A. Kyratzis, & J. Guo (Eds.), *Social interaction, social context, and language: Essays in honor of Susan Ervin-Tripp* (pp. 21–36). Hillsdale, NJ: Erlbaum.

Esposito, G., Setoh, P., Shinohara, K., & Bornstein, M. H. (2017). The development of attachment: Integrating genes, brain, behavior, and environment. *Behavioural Brain Research, 325,* 87–89. https://doi.org/10.1016/j.bbr.2017.03.025

Falkum, I. L. (2019). Pragmatic development: Learning to use language to communicate. In J. S. Horst & J. von Koss Torkildsen (Eds.), *International handbook of language acquisition* (pp. 234–260). New York: Taylor & Francis Group.

Farroni, T., Csibra, G., Simion, F., & Johnson, M. H. (2002). Eye contact detection in humans from birth. *Proceedings of the National Academy of*

*Sciences of the United States of America*, *99*, 9602–9605. https://doi.org/10 .1073/pnas.152159999

Fass, P. S. (2007). *Children of a new world: Society, culture, and globalization*. New York: New York University Press.

Feinman, S. (1992). *Social referencing and the social construction of reality in infancy*. New York: Plenum Press.

Feldman, D. H., & Morelock, M. J. (2011). Prodigies and savants. In R. J. Sternberg & S. B. Kaufman (Eds.), *The Cambridge handbook of intelligence* (pp. 210–234). New York: Cambridge University Press. https:// doi.org/10.1017/CBO9780511977244.012

Fenson, L., Dale, P. S., Reznick, S. J. et al. (1994). Variability in early communicative development. *Monographs of the Society for Research in Child Development*, *59* (Serial No. 242), 1–73. https://psycnet.apa.org/doi/10 .2307/1166093

Fields-Olivieri, M. A., Cole, P. M., & Roben, C. K. P. (2020). Toddler emotion expressions and emotional traits: Associations with parent-toddler verbal conversation. *Infant Behavior and Development*, *61*, 1–14. https://doi.org/10 .1016/j.infbeh.2020.101474

Fisher, A. V., Godwin, K. E., & Seltman, H. (2014). Visual environment, attention allocation, and learning in young children: When too much of a good thing may be bad. *Psychological Sciences*, *25*, 1362–1370. https://doi .org/10.1177%2F0956797614533801

Fitneva, S. A., & Matsui, T. (2015). The emergence and development of language across cultures. In L. A. Jensen (Ed.), *The Oxford handbook of human development and culture* (pp. 111–126). Oxford: Oxford University Press.

Fivush, R. (2014). Maternal reminiscing style: The sociocultural construction of autobiographical memory across childhood and adolescence. In P. J. Bauer & R. Fivush (Eds.), *The Wiley handbook on the development of children's memory* (pp. 568–585). Chichester: Wiley-Blackwell.

Fivush, R., Haden, C. A., & Reese, E. (1996). Remembering, recounting and reminiscing: The development of autobiographical memory in social context. In D. Rubin (Ed.), *Reconstructing our past: An overview of autobiographical memory* (pp. 341–359). New York: Cambridge University Press.

Fivush, R., & Hamond, N. R. (1989). Time and again: Effects of repetition and retention interval on two-year-olds' event recall. *Journal of Experimental Child Psychology*, *47*, 259–273. https://psycnet.apa.org/doi/10.1016/0022-0965(89)90032-5

Fivush, R., & Sales, J. M. (2004). Children's memory of emotional events. In D. Reisberg & P. Hertel (Eds.), *Memory and emotion* (pp. 242–271). New York: Oxford University Press.

Flavell, J. H. (1970). Developmental studies of mediated memory. In H. W. Reese & L. P. Lipsett (Eds.), *Advances in child development and child behavior* (Vol. 5, pp. 181–211). New York: Academic Press.

Flavell, J. H. (1984). Discussion. In R. J. Sternberg (Ed.), *Mechanisms of cognitive development* (pp. 187–209). New York: Freeman.

Flavell, J. H., Beach, D. R., & Chinsky, J. M. (1966). Spontaneous verbal rehearsal in a memory task as a function of age. *Child Development, 37,* 283–299. https://psycnet.apa.org/doi/10.2307/1126804

Flavell, J. H., Green, F. L., & Flavell, E. R. (1983). Development of knowledge about the appearance-reality distinction. *Monographs of the Society for Research in Child Development, 51*(1) (Serial No. 211), 1–68. https://psycnet.apa.org/doi/10.1016/0010-0285(83)90005-1

Flynn, E. (2010). Underpinning collaborative learning. In B. W. Sokol, U. Müller, J. M. Carpendale, A. R. Young, & G. Iarocci (Eds.), *Self and social regulation: Social interaction and the development of social understanding and executive functions* (pp. 312–336). New York: Oxford University Press.

Friedman, S. L., Scholnick, E. K., Bender, R. H. et al. (2014). Planning in middle childhood: Early predictors and later outcomes. *Child Development, 85,* 1446–1460. https://doi.org/10.1111/cdev.12221

Galluccio, L., & Rovee-Collier, C. (2007). Nonuniform effects of reinstatement within the time window. *Learning and Motivation, 37,* 1–17. https://doi.org/10.1016/j.lmot.2005.01.002

Garton, A. F. (2004). *Exploring cognitive development: The child as problem solver.* Malden, MA: Blackwell.

Gaskins, S., & Paradise, R. (2010). Learning through observation in daily life. In D. F. Lancy, J. Bock, & S. Gaskins (Eds.), *The anthropology of learning in childhood* (pp. 85–117). Walnut Creek, CA: Alta Mira Press.

Gauvain, M. (2001). *The social context of cognitive development.* New York: Guilford.

Gauvain, M. (2005). Scaffolding in socialization. *New Ideas in Psychology, 23,* 129–139. https://doi.org/10.1016/j.newideapsych.2006.05.004

Gauvain, M. (2009). Social and cultural transactions in cognitive development: A cross-generational view. In A. Sameroff (Ed.), *The transactional model of development: How children and contexts shape each other* (pp. 163–182). Washington, DC: American Psychological Association.

Gauvain, M. (2014). Geospatial tools and the changing nature of human spatial thinking. *Human Development*, *57*, 58–63. https://doi.org/10.1159/000358845

Gauvain, M. (2016). Peer contributions to cognitive development. In K. R. Wentzel & G. B. Ramani (Eds.), *Handbook of social influences in school contexts: Social-emotional, motivation, and cognitive outcomes* (pp. 80–95). New York: Taylor & Francis Group.

Gauvain, M., & Nicolaides, C. (2015). Cognition in childhood across cultures. In L. A. Jensen (Ed.), *The Oxford handbook of human development and culture: An interdisciplinary perspective* (pp. 198–213). New York: Oxford University Press.

Gauvain, M., & Perez, S. M. (2015). Cognitive development and culture. In R. M. Lerner (Series Ed.) and L. Liben & U. Müller (Vol. Eds.), *Handbook of child psychology and developmental science: Cognitive processes* (7th ed., Vol. 2, pp. 854–896). New York: Wiley.

Gauvain, M., Perez, S. M., & Reisz, Z. (2018). Stability and change in mother-child planning over middle childhood. *Developmental Psychology*, *54*, 571–585. https://doi.org/10.1037/dev0000456

Gauvain, M., & Reynolds, C. A. (2011). The sociocultural context of cognition across the life span. In K. L. Fingerman, C. A. Berg, J. Smith, & T. C. Antonucci (Eds.), *Handbook of life-span development* (pp. 269–297). New York: Springer.

Gergely, G., Bekkering, H., & Kiraly, I. (2002). Rational imitation in pre-verbal infants. *Nature*, *415*, 755. https://psycnet.apa.org/doi/10.1038/415755a

Goldin-Meadows, S. (2015). Gesture and cognitive development. In R. M. Lerner (Series Ed. ) and L. Liben & U. Müller (Vol. Eds.), *Handbook of child psychology and developmental science: Cognitive processes* (7th ed., Vol. 2, pp. 339–380). New York: Wiley.

Golinkoff, R. M., Hirsh-Pasek, K., Bailey, L. M., & Wenger, N. R. (1992). Young children and adults use lexical principles to learn new words. *Developmental Psychology*, *28*, 99–108. https://psycnet.apa.org/doi/10.1037/0012-1649.28.1.99

Göncü, A., Jain, J., & Tuermer, U. (2007). Children's play as cultural interpretation. In A. Göncü & S. Gaskins (Eds.), *Play and development: Evolutionary, sociocultural, and functional perspectives* (pp. 155–178). Mahwah, NJ: Erlbaum.

Goodnow, J. J. (1990). The socialization of cognition: What's involved? In J. W. Stigler, R. A. Shweder, & G. Herdt (Eds.), *Cultural psychology: Essays on comparative human development* (pp. 259–286). Cambridge: Cambridge University Press.

Goodnow, J. J. (2010). Culture. In M. H. Bornstein (Ed.), *Handbook of cultural developmental science* (pp. 3–19). New York: Psychology Press.

Goodnow, J. J., Miller, P. J., & Kessel, F. (1995). *Cultural practices as contexts for development*. San Francisco, CA: Jossey-Bass.

Gopnik, A., & Astington, J. W. (1988). Children's understanding of representational change and its relation to the understanding of false belief. *Child Development, 59*, 26–37. https://doi.org/10.2307/1130386

Gopnik, A., Meltzoff, A. N., & Kuhl, P. K. (1999). *The scientist in the crib: Minds, brains, and how children learn*. New York: Harper Collins.

Goswami, U. (1995). Transitive relational mappings in three- and four-year-olds: The analogy of Goldilocks and the Three Bears. *Child Development, 66*, 877–892. https://doi.org/10.1111/j.1467-8624.1995.tb00911.x

Goswami, U., & Brown, A. L. (1990). Higher-order structure and relational reasoning: Contrasting analogical and thematic relations. *Cognition, 36*, 207–226. https://doi.org/10.1016/0010-0277(90)90057-Q

Gottlieb, G. (1992). *Individual development and evolution: The genesis of novel behavior*. New York: Oxford University Press.

Gottlieb, G. (1997). *Synthesizing nature-nurture*. Mahwah, NJ: Erlbaum.

Gottlieb, G. (2007). Probabilistic epigenesis. *Developmental Science, 10*, 1–11. https://doi.org/10.1111/j.1467-7687.2007.00556.x

Greenfield, P. M. (2009). Linking social change and developmental change: Shifting pathways of human development. *Developmental Psychology, 45*, 401–418. https://psycnet.apa.org/doi/10.1037/a0014726

Greenough, W. T., Black, J. E., & Wallace, C. S. (1987). Experience and brain development. *Child Development, 58*, 539–559. https://psycnet.apa.org/doi/10.2307/1130197

Hackman, D. A., Farah, M. J., & Meaney, M. J. (2010). Socioeconomic status and the brain: Mechanistic insights from human and animal research. *Nature Reviews Neuroscience, 11*, 651–659. https://doi.org/10.1038/nrn2897

Haden, C. A., & Ornstein, P. A. (2009). Research on talking about the past: The past, present, and future. *Journal of Cognition and Development, 10*, 135–142. https://doi.org/10.1080/15248370903155718

Haden, C. A., Ornstein, P. A., Eckerman, C. O., & Didow, S. M. (2001). Mother–child conversational interactions as events unfold: Linkages to subsequent remembering. *Child Development, 72*, 1016–1031. https://doi.org/10.1111/1467-8624.00332

Haden, C. A., Ornstein, P. A., O'Brien, B. S. et al. (2011). The development of children's early memory skills. *Journal of Experimental Child Psychology, 108*, 44–60. https://doi.org/10.1016/j.jecp.2010.06.007

Hamlin, J. K., Wynn, K., & Bloom, P. (2007). Social evaluation of preverbal infants. *Nature*, *450*, 557–559. https://doi.org/10.1038/nature06288

Hammond, S. I., Müller, U., Carpendale, J. M., Bibok, M. B., & Liebermann-Finestone, D. P. (2012). The effects of parental scaffolding on preschoolers' executive function. *Developmental Psychology*, *48*(1), 271–281. https://psycnet.apa.org/doi/10.1037/a0025519

Harkness, S., & Super, C. M. (2020). Cross-cultural research on parents: Applications to the care and development of children. *New Directions for Child and Adolescent Development*. Hoboken, NJ: Wiley.

Harris, P. L., Koenig, M. A., Corriveau, K. H., & Jaswal, V. K. (2018). Cognitive foundations of learning from testimony. *Annual Review of Psychology*, *69*, 251–273. https://doi.org/10.1146/annurev-psych-122216-011710

Hawkins, J., Pea, R. D., Glick, J., & Scribner, S. (1984). "Merds that laugh don't like mushrooms": Evidence for deductive reasoning by preschoolers. *Developmental Psychology*, *20*, 584–594. https://psycnet.apa.org/doi/10.1037/0012-1649.20.4.584

Heckhaussen, J. (2000). Evolutionary perspectives on human motivation. *American Behavioral Scientist*, *43*, 1015–1029. https://doi.org/10.1177%2F00027640021955739

Hinde, R. A. (1989). Ethological and relationships perspectives. In R. Vasta (Ed.), *Annals of child development* (Vol. 6, pp. 251–285). Greenwich, CT: JAI Press.

Hitch, G. J., & Towse, J. N. (1995). Working memory: What develops? In F. E. Weinert & W. Schneider (Eds.), *Memory performance and competencies: Issues in growth and development* (pp. 3–21). Mahwah, NJ: Erlbaum.

Hoff, E. (2015a). Language development. In M. H. Bornstein & M. E. Lamb (Eds.), *Developmental science: An advanced textbook* (pp. 443–488). New York: Taylor & Francis.

Hoff, E. (2015b). Language development in bilingual children. In E. Bavin and L. Naigles (Eds.), *The Cambridge handbook of child language* (pp. 483–503). Cambridge: Cambridge University Press.

Hoff, E. (2018). Bilingual development in children of immigrant families. *Child Development Perspectives*, *12*, 80–86. https://doi.org/10.1111/cdep.12303

Holmes, C. J., Kim-Spoon, J., & Deater-Dekard, K. (2016). Linking executive function and peer problems from early childhood through middle adolescence. *Journal of Abnormal Child Psychology*, *44*, 31–42. https://doi.org/10.1007/s10802-015-0044-5

Holowka, S., Brosseau-Lapré, F., & Petitto, L. A. (2002). Semantic and conceptual knowledge underlying bilingual babies' first signs and words.

*Language Learning*, *52*(2), 205–262. https://doi.org/10.1111/0023-8333.00184

Homer, B. D., & Tamis-LeMonda, C. S. (2012). *The development of social cognition and communication*. East Sussex: Psychology Press.

Howe, M. L. (2014). The co-emergence of the self and autobiographical memory: An adaptive view of early memory. In P. J. Bauer & R. Fivush (Eds.), *The Wiley handbook on the development of children's memory* (Vol. 2, pp. 545–567). Chichester: Wiley-Blackwell.

Howe, M. L. (2015). Memory development. In R. M. Lerner (Series Ed.) and L. Liben & U. Müller (Vol. Eds.), *Handbook of child psychology and developmental science: Cognitive processes* (7th ed., Vol. 2, pp. 203–249). New York: Wiley.

Howe, M. L., Courage, M. L., & Edison, S. C. (2003). When autobiographical memory begins. *Developmental Review*, *23*, 471–494. https://psycnet.apa.org/doi/10.1016/j.dr.2003.09.001

Hudson, J. A. (1990). The emergence of autobiographical memory in mother-child conversation. In R. Fivush & J. A. Hudson (Eds.), *Knowing and remembering in young children* (pp. 166–196). New York: Cambridge University Press.

Hudson, J. A., & Grysman, A. (2014). Extending the life of a memory: Effects of reminders on children's long-term event memory. In P. J. Bauer & R. Fivush (Eds.), *The Wiley handbook on the development of children's memory* (pp. 255–284). Chichester: Wiley-Blackwell.

Hunter, M. A., & Ames, E. W. (1988). A multifactor model of infant preferences for novel and familiar stimuli. In C. Rovee-Collier & L. P. Lipsitt (Eds.), *Advances in infancy research* (Vol. 5, pp. 69–95). New York: Ablex.

Huttenlocher, J., Smiley, P., & Charney, R. (1987). Emergence of action categories in the child: Evidence from verb meanings. *Psychological Review*, *90*, 72–93. https://psycnet.apa.org/doi/10.1037/0033-295X.90.1.72

Huttenlocher, J., Waterfall, H., Vasilyeva, N., Vevea, J., & Hedges, L. V. (2010). Sources of variability in children's language growth. *Cognitive Psychology*, *61*, 343–365. https://doi.org/10.1016/j.cogpsych.2010.08.002

Hyams, N., & Orfitelli, R. (2018). The acquisition of syntax. In E. M. Fernandez & H. S. Cairns (Eds.), *The handbook of psycholinguistics* (pp. 593–614). Hoboken, NJ: Wiley-Blackwell.

Jablonka, E., & Lamb, M. J. (2007). Précis of evolution in four dimensions. *Behavioral and Brain Sciences*, *30*, 353–392. https://doi.org/10.1017/S0140525X07002221

Johnson, M. H. (2005). Sub-cortical face processing. *Nature Reviews Neuroscience*, *6*, 766–774. https://doi.org/10.1038/nrn1766

Johnson, M. H. (2011). Interactive specialization: A domain-general framework for human functional brain development? *Developmental Cognitive Neuroscience, 1*(1), 7–21. https://doi.org/10.1016/j.dcn.2010.07.003

Johnson, N. H., & de Haan, M. (2015). *Developmental cognitive neuroscience: An introduction* (4th ed.). Malden, MA: Wiley-Blackwell.

Johnson, S. P., & Hannon, E. E. (2015). Perceptual development. In R. M. Lerner (Series Ed.) and L. Liben & U. Müller (Vol. Eds.), *Handbook of child psychology and developmental science: Cognitive processes* (7th ed., Vol. 2, pp. 63–112). New York: Wiley.

Joiner, R., Littleton, K., Faulkner, D., & Miell, D. (2000). *Rethinking collaborative learning*. London: Free Association Books.

Kail, R. (2000). Speed of information processing: Developmental change and links to intelligence. *Journal of School Psychology, 38*, 51–61. https://psycnet.apa.org/doi/10.1016/S0022-4405(99)00036-9

Kail, R. V. (2007). Longitudinal evidence that increases in processing speed and working memory enhance children's reasoning. *Psychological Science, 18*, 312–313. https://psycnet.apa.org/doi/10.1111/j.1467-9280.2007.01895.x

Kail, R. V., & Ferrer, E. F. (2007). Processing speed in childhood and adolescence: Longitudinal models for examining developmental change. *Child Development, 78*, 1760–1770. https://doi.org/10.1111/j.1467-8624.2007.01088.x

Kail, R. V., McBride-Chang, C., Ferrer, E., Cho, J.-R., & Shu, H. (2013). Cultural differences in the development of processing speed. *Developmental Science, 16*, 476–483. https://doi.org/10.1111/desc.12039

Kaller, C. P., Rahm, B., Spreer, J., Mader, I., & Unterrainer, J. M. (2008). Thinking around the corner: The development of planning abilities. *Brain and Cognition, 67*, 360–370. https://doi.org/10.1016/j.bandc.2008.02.003

Karasik, L. B., Tamis-LeMonda, C. S., Adolph, K. E., & Bornstein, M. H. (2015). Places and posture: A cross-cultural comparison of sitting in 5-month-olds. *Journal of Cross-Cultural Psychology, 46*, 1023–1038. https://doi.org/10.1177/0022022115593803

Kearins, J. (1981). Visual spatial memory in Aboriginal and white Australian children. *Cognitive Psychology, 13*, 434–460. https://psycnet.apa.org/doi/10.1016/0010-0285(81)90017-7

Kee, D. W. (1994). Developmental differences in associative memory: Strategy use, mental effort, and knowledge-access interaction. In H. W. Reese (Ed.), *Advances in child development and behavior* (Vol. 25, pp. 7–32). New York: Academic Press.

Kellman, P. J., & Arterberry, M. E. (2006). Infant visual perception. In W. Damon & R. M. Lerner (Series Eds.) and D. Kuhn & R. S. Siegler

(Vol. Eds.), *Handbook of child psychology: Cognition, perception, and language* (6th ed., Vol. 2, pp. 109–160). New York: Wiley.

Kent, R. (2005). Speech development. In B. Hopkins (Ed.), *The Cambridge encyclopedia of child development* (pp. 257–264). New York: Cambridge University Press.

Kessen, W. (1960). Research design in the study of developmental problems. In P. H. Mussen (Ed.), *Handbook of research methods in child development* (pp. 36–70). New York: John Wiley.

Kisilevsky, B. S., Hains, S. M. J., Lee, K. et al. (2003). Effects of experience on fetal voice recognition. *Psychological Science, 14*, 220–224. https://doi.org/10.1111/1467-9280.02435

Klahr, D. (2000). *Exploring science: The cognition and development of discovery processes*. Cambridge, MA: MIT Press.

Klahr, D., Zimmerman, C., & Jirout, J. (2011). Educational interventions to advance children's scientific thinking. *Science, 333*, 971–975. https://psycnet.apa.org/doi/10.1126/science.1204528

Koenig, M. A., Li, P. H., & McMyler, B. (2021). Interpersonal trust in children's testimonial learning. *Mind & Language*, 1–20. https://doi.org/10.1111/mila.12361

Konner, M. J. (2010). *The evolution of childhood: Relationships, emotion, mind*. Cambridge, MA: Belknap Press.

Kubicek, L. F., & Emde, R. N. (2012). Emotional expression and language: A longitudinal study of typically developing earlier and later talkers from 15 to 30 months. *Infant Mental Health Journal, 33*, 553–584. https://doi.org/10.1002/imhj.21365

Kuhl, P. K. (2009). Early language acquisition: Phonetic and word learning, neural substrates, and a theoretical model. In B. Moore, L. Tyler, & W. Marslen-Wilson (Eds.), *The perception of speech: From sound to meaning* (pp. 103–131). Oxford: Oxford University Press.

Kwon, A. Y., Vallotton, C. D., Kiegelmann, M., & Wilhelm, K. H. (2018). Cultural diversification of communicative gestures through early childhood: A comparison of children in English-, German-, and Chinese- speaking families. *Infant Behavior and Development, 50*, 328–339. https://doi.org/10.1016/j.infbeh.2017.10.003

Lancy, D. (2008). *The anthropology of childhood: Cherubs, chattel, changelings*. Cambridge: Cambridge University Press.

Lerner, R. M., Hershberg, R. M., Hilliard, L. J., & Johnson, S. K. (2015). Concepts and theories of human development. In M. H. Bornstein & M. E. Lamb (Eds.), *Developmental science: An advanced textbook* (pp. 3–41). New York: Taylor & Francis.

Lewis, M., & Brooks-Gunn, J. (1979). *Social cognition and the acquisition of the self.* New York: Plenum Press.

Liben, L. S. (2009). The road to understanding maps. *Current Directions in Psychological Science, 18,* 310–315. https://psycnet.apa.org/doi/10.1111/j .1467-8721.2009.01658.x

Liben, L. S., & Christensen, A. E. (2011). Spatial development: Evolving approaches to enduring questions. In U. Goswami (Ed.), *The Wiley-Blackwell handbook of childhood cognitive development* (2nd ed., pp. 446–472). Malden, MA: Wiley-Blackwell.

Liben, L. S., & Downs, R. M. (2015). Map use skills. In M. Monmonier (Ed.), *Cartography in the twentieth century* (pp. 1074–1080). Chicago, IL: University of Chicago Press.

Lickliter, R., & Honeycutt, H. (2015). Biology, development, and human systems. In R. Lerner (Series Ed.) and W. F. Overton & P. C. M. Molenaar (Vol. Eds.), *Handbook of child psychology and developmental science: Theory and method* (7th ed., Vol. 1, pp. 162–207). New York: Wiley.

Liddle, B., & Nettle, D. (2006). Higher-order theory of mind and social competence in school-age children. *Journal of Cultural and Evolutionary Psychology, 4*(3–4), 231–244. https://doi.org/10.1556/JCEP.4.2006.3-4.3

Lillard, A. S. (2015). The development of play. In R. M. Lerner (Series Ed.) and L. Liben & U. Müller (Vol. Eds.), *Handbook of child psychology and developmental science: Cognitive processes* (7th ed., Vol. 2, pp. 425–468). New York: Wiley.

Liszkowski, U., Brown, P., Callaghan, T., Takada, A., & de Vos, C. (2012). A prelinguistic gestural universal of human communication. *Cognitive Science, 36,* 698–713. https://doi.org/10.1111/j.1551-6709.2011.01228.x

Lukowski, A. F., & Bauer, P. J. (2014). Long-term memory in infancy and early childhood. In P. J. Bauer & R. Fivush (Eds.), *The Wiley handbook on the development of children's memory* (Vol. 1, pp. 230–254). Chichester: Wiley-Blackwell.

Lyons, K. E., & Ghetti, S. (2010). Metacognitive development in early childhood: New questions about old assumptions. In A. Efklides & P. Misailidi (Eds.), *Trends and prospects in metacognition research* (pp. 259–278). New York: Springer. www.proquest.com/books/metacognitive-development-early-childhood-new/docview/761417245/se-2?accountid=14521

Lyons, K. E., & Zelazo, P. D. (2011). Monitoring, metacognition, and executive function: Elucidating the role of self-reflection in the development of self-regulation. In J. Benson (Ed.), *Advances in child development and behavior* (Vol. 40, pp. 379–412). Burlington: Academic Press.

MacWhinney, B. (2015). Language development. In R. M. Lerner (Series Ed.) and L. Liben & U. Müller (Vol. Eds.), *Handbook of child psychology and developmental science: Cognitive processes* (7th ed., Vol. 2, pp. 296–338). New York: Wiley.

Maddieson, I. (2005). Consonant inventories. In M. Haspelmath, M. S. Dryer, D. Gil, & B. Comrie (Eds.), *The world atlas of language structures* (pp. 10–14). Oxford: Oxford University Press.

Manian, N., & Bornstein, M. H. (2009). Dynamics of emotion in infants of clinically depressed and nondepressed mothers. *Journal of Child Psychology and Psychiatry*, *50*, 1410–1418. https://doi.org/10.1111/j.1469-7610 .2009.02166.x

Maphalala, Z., Pascoe, M., & Smouse, M. R. (2014). Phonological development of first language isiXhosa-speaking children aged 3;0–6;0 years: A descriptive cross-sectional study. *Clinical Linguistics and Phonetics*, *28*, 174–194. https://doi.org/10.3109/02699206.2013.840860

Mareschal, D., Johnson, M. H., Sirois, S. et al. (2007). *Neoconstructivism: How the brain constructs cognition.* Oxford: Oxford University Press.

Markman, E. M. (2014). Constraints on word learning: Speculations about their nature, origins, and domain specificity. In M. R. Gunnar & M. Maratsos (Eds.), *Modularity and constraints in language and cognition* (pp. 59–102). New York: Psychology Press.

Marshall, P. J., & Shipley, T. F. (2009). Event-related potentials to point-light displays of human actions in 5-month-old infants. *Developmental Neuropsychology*, *34*, 368–377. https://doi.org/10.1080/87565640902801866

Maslen, R. J. C., Theakston, A. L., Lieven, E. V. M., & Tomasello, M. (2004). A dense corpus study of past tense and overregularization in English. *Journal of Speech, Language, and Hearing Research*, *47*, 1319–1333. https://psycnet .apa.org/doi/10.1044/1092-4388(2004/099)

Maurer, D., & Salapatek, P. (1976). Developmental changes in the scanning of faces by young infants. *Child Development*, *47*, 523–527. https://psycnet .apa.org/doi/10.2307/1128813

Maynard, A. E., Subrahmanyam, K., & Greenfield, P. M. (2005). Technology and the development of intelligence: From the loom to the computer. In R. J. Sternberg & D. D. Preiss (Eds.), *Intelligence and technology: The impact of tools on the nature and development of human abilities* (pp. 29–53). Hillsdale, NJ: Erlbaum.

McBride-Chang, C., Zhou, Y., Cho, J.-C. et al. (2011). Visual spatial skills: A consequence of learning to read? *Journal of Experimental Child Psychology*, *109*, 256–262. https://doi.org/10.1016/j.jecp.2010.12.003

McCormack, T., & Atance, C. M. (2011). Planning in young children: A review and synthesis. *Developmental Review*, *31*, 1–31. https://doi.org/10.1016/j .dr.2011.02.002

Mead, M. (1955). *Childhood in contemporary cultures*. Chicago, IL: University of Chicago Press.

Meaney, M. J. (2010). Epigenetics and the biological definition of gene × environment interactions. *Child Development*, *81*(1), 41–79. https://doi.org/ 10.1111/j.1467-8624.2009.01381.x

Miller, P. H. (2016). *Theories of developmental psychology* (6th ed.). New York: Worth.

Miller, P. J., Fung, H., Lin, S., Chen, E. C.-H., & Boldt, B. R. (2012). How socialization happens on the ground: Narrative practices as alternate socializing pathways in Taiwanese and European-American families. *Monographs of the Society for Research in Child Development*, *77* (Serial No. 302), 77–104. DOI:10.1111/j.1540-5834.2011.00646.x

Mistry, J., Contreras, M., & Dutta, R. (2013). Culture and child development. In R. M. Lerner, M. Easterbrooks, & J. Mistry (Eds.), *Handbook of psychology: Developmental psychology* (2nd ed., Vol. 6, pp. 265–285). Editor-in-Chief: I. B. Weiner. Hoboken, NJ: Wiley.

Mondloch, C. J., Lewis, T. L., Budreau, D. et al. (1999). Face perception during early infancy. *Psychological Science*, *10*, 419–422. https://psycnet.apa.org/ doi/10.1111/1467-9280.00179

Moore, D. S. (2015). *The developing gene: The fallacy of "nature vs. nurture."* New York: Freeman.

Mpogole, H., Hidaya, U., & Tedre, M. (January 15–16, 2008). Mobile phones and poverty alleviation: A survey study in rural Tanzania. *Proceedings of 1st International Conference on M4D Mobile Communication Technology for Development*. Iringa, Tanzania.

Müller, U., & Kerns, K. (2015). The development of executive function. In R. M. Lerner (Series Ed.) and L. Liben & U. Müller (Vol. Eds.), *Handbook of child psychology and developmental science: Cognitive processes* (7th ed., Vol. 2, pp. 425–468). New York: Wiley.

Munakata, Y. (2006). Information processing approaches to development. In W. Damon & R. M. Lerner (Series Eds.) and D. Kuhn & R. S. Siegler (Vol. Eds.), *Handbook of child psychology: Cognition, perception, and language* (6th ed., Vol. 2, pp. 426–463). New York: Wiley.

Nakamura, K. (2001). The acquisition of polite language by Japanese children. In K. E. Nelson, A. Aksu-Koc, & C. E. Johnson (Eds.), *Children's language: Developing narrative and discourse competence* (pp. 93–112). Mahwah, NJ: Erlbaum.

National Academies of Sciences, Engineering, and Medicine. (2018). *How people learn II: Learners, contexts, and cultures*. Washington, DC: The National Academies Press.

National Academies of Sciences, Engineering, and Medicine. (2021). *Science and engineering in preschool through elementary grades: The brilliance of children and the strengths of educators*. Washington, DC: The National Academies Press. https://doi.org/10.17226/26215.

Naus, M. J. (1982). Memory development in the young reader: The combined effects of knowledge base and memory processing. In W. Otto & S. White (Eds.), *Reading expository material* (pp. 49–74). New York: Academic Press.

Nelson, C. A., Thomas, K. M., & de Haan, M. (2006). Neural basis of cognitive development. In W. Damon & R. M. Lerner (Series Eds.) and D. Kuhn & R. S. Siegler (Vol. Eds.), *Handbook of child psychology: Cognition, perception, and language* (6th ed., Vol. 2, pp. 3–57). New York: Wiley.

Nelson, K. (2014). Sociocultural theories of memory development. In P. J. Bauer & R. Fivush (Eds.), *The Wiley handbook on the development of children's memory* (pp. 87–108). Chichester: Wiley-Blackwell.

Niebaum, J., & Munakata, Y. (2020). Deciding what to do: Developments in children's spontaneous monitoring of cognitive demands. *Child Development Perspectives*, *14*, 202–207. https://doi.org/10.1111/cdep.12383

Ninio, A., & Snow, C. E. (1999). The development of pragmatics: Learning to use language appropriately. In W. C. Ritchie & T. K. Bhatia (Eds.), *Handbook of child language acquisition* (pp. 347–383). San Diego, CA: Academic Press.

Oakes, L. M., & Tellinghuisen, D. J. (1994). Examining in infancy: Does it reflect active processing? *Developmental Psychology*, *30*, 748–756. https://psycnet.apa.org/doi/10.1037/0012-1649.30.5.748

Ochs, E., & Schieffelin, B. (2016). *Acquiring conversational competence*. London: Routledge.

Onishi, K. H., & Baillargeon, R. (2005). Do 15-month-old infants understand false belief? *Science*, *308*, 352–359. https://doi.org/10.1126%2Fscience.1107621

Ornstein, P. A., & Coffman, J. (2020). Toward an understanding of the development of skilled remembering: The role of teachers' instructional language. *Current Directions in Psychological Science*, *29*, 445–452. https://doi.org/10.1177%2F0963721420925543

Ornstein, P. A., Naus, M. J., & Liberty, C. (1975). Rehearsal and organizational processes in children's memory. *Child Development*, *46*, 818–830. https://psycnet.apa.org/doi/10.2307/1128385

Overton, W. F. (1984). World views and their influence on psychological theory and research: Kuhn-Lakotos-Lauden. In H. W. Reese (Ed.), *Advances in child development and behavior* (Vol. 18, pp. 191–226). Orlando, FL: Academic Press.

Packer, M., & Cole, M. (2015). Culture in development. In M. H. Bornstein & M. E. Lamb (Eds.), *Developmental science: An advanced textbook* (pp. 43–111). New York: Taylor & Francis.

Parrish-Morris, J., Golinkoff, R. M., & Hirsh-Pasek, K. (2013). From coo to code: A brief story of language development. In P. D. Zelazo (Ed.), *The Oxford handbook of developmental psychology* (Vol. 1, pp. 867–908). New York: Oxford University Press.

Pascalis, O., de Haan, M., & Nelson, C. A. (2002). Is face processing species-specific during the first year of life? *Science, 5*, 427–434. https://psycnet.apa.org/doi/10.1126/science.1070223

Paulus, M. (2011). How infants relate looker and object: Evidence for a perceptual learning account of gaze following in infancy. *Developmental Science, 14*, 1301–1310. https://doi.org/10.1111/j.1467-7687.2011.01076.x

Pearson, B. Z., Fernandez, S. C., Lewedeg, V., & Oller, D. K. (1997). The relation of input factors of lexical learning by bilingual infants (ages 8 to 30 months). *Applied Psycholinguistics, 18*, 41–58. https://psycnet.apa.org/doi/10.1017/S0142716400009863

Peisner-Feinberg, E. S., Burchinal, M. R., Clifford, R. M. et al. (2001). The relation of preschool child-care quality to children's cognitive and social developmental trajectories through second grade. *Child Development, 72*, 1534–1553. https://doi.org/10.1111/1467-8624.00364

Peterson, L. R., & Peterson, M. J. (1959). Short-term retention of individual verbal items. *Journal of Experimental Psychology, 58*, 193–198. https://psycnet.apa.org/doi/10.1037/h0049234

Piaget, J. (1926). *The language and thought of the child.* New York: Harcourt, Brace.

Piaget, J. (1929). *The child's conception of the world.* New York: Harcourt, Brace.

Pinker, S. (2007). *The language instinct.* New York: Harper.

Pressley, M., & Hilden, K. (2006). Cognitive strategies. In W. Damon & R. M. Lerner (Series Eds.) and D. Kuhn & R. S. Siegler (Vol. Eds.), *Handbook of child psychology: Cognition, perception, and language* (6th ed., Vol. 2, pp. 511–556). Hoboken, NJ: Wiley.

Putnick, D. L., & Bornstein, M. H. (2016). Girls' and boys' labor and household chores in low- and middle-income countries. In M. H. Bornstein, D. L. Putnick, J. E. Lansford, K. Deater-Deckard, & R. H. Bradley (Eds.),

Gender in low- and middle-income countries. *Monograph of the Society for Research in Child Development, 81*(1) (Serial No. 320), 104–122. https://doi.org/10.1111/mono.12228

Redshaw, J., Vandersee, J., Bulley, A., & Gilbert, S. (2018). Development of children's use of external reminders for hard-to-remember intentions. *Child Development, 89*, 2099–2108. https://doi.org/10.1111/cdev.13040

Reese, E. (2019). Language learning from books. In J. S. Horst & J. von Koss Torkildsen (Eds.), *International handbook of language acquisition* (pp. 462–484). New York: Taylor & Francis Group.

Reznick, J. S. (2014). Methodological challenges in the study of short-term working memory in infants. In P. J. Bauer & R. Fivush (Eds.), *The Wiley handbook on the development of children's memory* (Vol. 1, pp. 230–254). Chichester: Wiley-Blackwell.

Ricco, R. R. (2015). The development of reasoning. In R. M. Lerner (Series Ed.) and L. Liben & U. Müller (Vol. Eds.), *Handbook of child psychology and developmental science: Cognitive processes* (7th ed., Vol. 2, pp. 519–570). New York: Wiley.

Richards, J. E., & Anderson, D. E. (2004). Attentional inertia in children's extended looking at television. In R. V. Kail (Ed.), *Advances in child development and behavior* (Vol. 32, pp. 163–212). San Diego, CA: Elsevier.

Richert, R. A., & Lillard, A. S. (2002). Children's understanding of the knowledge prerequisites of drawing and pretending. *Developmental Psychology, 38*, 1004–1015. https://psycnet.apa.org/doi/10.1037/0012-1649.38.6.1004

Richland, L. E., Morrison, R. G., & Holyoak, K. J. (2006). Children's development of analogical reasoning: Insights from scene analogy problems. *Journal of Experimental Child Psychology, 94*, 249–273. https://doi.org/10.1016/j.jecp.2006.02.002

Richland, L. E., Zur, O., & Holyoak, K. J. (2007). Cognitive supports for analogies in the mathematics classroom. *Science, 316*, 1128–1129. https://psycnet.apa.org/doi/10.1126/science.1142103

Rochat, P. (2015). Layers of awareness in development. *Developmental Review, 38*, 122–145. https://doi.org/10.1016/j.dr.2015.07.009

Rochat, P., & Striano, T. (2002). Who's in the mirror? Self-other discrimination in specular images by four- and nine-month-old infants. *Child Development, 73*, 35–46. https://doi.org/10.1111/1467-8624.00390

Rochat, P., & Zahavi, D. (2011). The uncanny mirror: A re-framing of mirror self-experience. *Cognition and Consciousness, 20*, 204–213. https://doi.org/10.1016/j.concog.2010.06.007

Roebers, C. M. (2017). Executive function and metacognition: Towards a unifying framework of cognitive self-regulation. *Developmental Review*, *45*, 31–51. https://doi.org/10.1016/j.dr.2017.04.001

Rogoff, B. (1990). *Apprenticeship in thinking: Cognitive development in social context*. New York: Oxford University Press.

Rogoff, B. (2003). *The cultural nature of human development*. New York: Oxford University Press.

Rogoff, B., Paradise, R., Arauz, R. M., Correa-Chávez, M., & Angelillo, C. (2003). Firsthand learning through intent participation. *Annual Review of Psychology*, *54*, 175–203. https://doi.org/10.1146/annurev.psych.54.101601.145118

Ronfard, S., & Lane, J. D. (2018). Preschoolers continually adjust their epistemic trust based on an informant's ongoing accuracy. *Child Development*, *89*, 414–429. https://doi.org/10.1111/cdev.12720

Rosa, A., & Valsiner, J. (2018). *The Cambridge handbook of sociocultural psychology*. New York: Cambridge University Press. https://doi.org/10.1017/9781316662229

Ross-Sheehy, S., Oakes, L. M., & Luck, S. J. (2003). The development of visual short-term memory capacity in infants. *Child Development*, *74*, 1807–1822. https://doi.org/10.1046/j.1467-8624.2003.00639.x

Rothbart, M. K., & Bates, J. (2006). Temperament. In W. Damon & R. M. Lerner (Gen. Eds.) and N. Eisenberg (Ed.), *Handbook of child psychology: Social, emotional, and personality development* (6th ed., Vol. 3, pp. 99–166). New York: Wiley.

Rothbart, M. K., Sheese, B. E., Rueda, M., & Posner, M. I. (2011). Developing mechanisms of self-regulation in early life. *Emotion Review*, *3*, 207–213. https://doi.org/10.1177%2F1754073910387943

Rovee-Collier, C. (1995). Time windows in cognitive development. *Developmental Psychology*, *31*, 147–169. https://psycnet.apa.org/doi/10.1037/0012-1649.31.2.147

Rovee-Collier, C., & Cuevas, K. (2009). Multiple memory systems are unnecessary to account for infant memory development: An ecological model. *Developmental Psychology*, *45*, 160–174. https://doi.org/10.1037%2Fa0014538

Rovee-Collier, C. K., & Shyi, G. (1992). A functional and cognitive analysis of infant long-term retention. In C. J. Brainard, M. L. Howe, & V. Reyna (Eds.), *Development of long-term retention* (pp. 3–55). New York: Springer-Verlag.

Ruff, H. A., & Capozzoli, M. C. (2003). Development of attention and distractibility in the first 4 years of life. *Developmental Psychology*, *39*, 877–890. https://psycnet.apa.org/doi/10.1037/0012-1649.39.5.877

Ruff, H. A., & Rothbart, M. K. (1996). *Attention in early development: Themes and variations*. New York: Oxford University Press.

Rutter, M. (2006). *Genes and behavior.* New York: Blackwell.

Saffran, J. R., Aslin, R. N., & Newport, E. L. (1996). Statistical learning by 8-month-old infants. *Science, 274,* 1926–1928. https://doi.org/10.1126/science.274.5294.1926

Saffran, J. R., Werker, J., & Werner, L. A. (2006). The infant's auditory world. In W. Damon & R. M. Lerner (Series Eds.) and D. Kuhn & R. S. Siegler (Vol. Eds.), *Handbook of child psychology: Cognition, perception, and language* (6th ed., Vol. 2, pp. 58–108). New York: Wiley.

Sameroff, A. (2009). The transactional model. In A. Sameroff (Ed.), *The transactional model of development: How children and contexts shape each other* (pp. 3–21). Washington, DC: American Psychological Association.

Sarnthein, J., vonStein, A., Rappelsberger, P. et al. (1997). Persistent patterns of brain activity: An EEG coherence study of the positive effect of music on spatial-temporal reasoning. *Neurological Research, 19,* 107–116. https://doi.org/10.1080/01616412.1997.11740782

Sawyer, R. K. (2014). *Cambridge handbook of the learning sciences* (2nd ed.). New York: Cambridge University Press.

Sayfan, L., & Lagattuta, K. H. (2009). Scaring the monster away: What children know about managing fears of real and imaginary creatures. *Child Development, 80,* 1756–1774. https://psycnet.apa.org/doi/10.1111/j.1467-8624.2009.01366.x

Schneider, J. L., & Iverson, J. M. (2021). Cascades in action: How the transition to walking shapes caregiver communication during everyday interactions. *Developmental Psychology, 58,* 1–16. https://psycnet.apa.org/doi/10.1037/dev0001280

Schneider, W. (2010). Memory development in childhood. In U. Goswami (Ed.), *Blackwell handbook of childhood cognitive development* (2nd ed., pp. 236–256). London: Blackwell.

Schneider, W. (2014). Individual differences in memory development and educational implications: Cross-sectional and longitudinal evidence. In P. J. Bauer & R. Fivush (Eds.), *The Wiley handbook on the development of children's memory* (Vol. 2, pp. 947–971). Chichester: Wiley.

Schneider, W. (2015). *Memory development from early childhood to adulthood.* New York: Springer.

Schneider, W., & Ornstein, P. A. (2015). The development of children's memory. *Child Development Perspectives, 9,* 190–195. https://doi.org/10.1111/cdep.12129

Schonert-Reichl, K. A., Oberle, E., Lawlor, M. S. et al. (2015). Enhancing cognitive and social-emotional development through a simple-to-administer mindfulness-based school program for elementary school children: A randomized controlled trial. *Developmental Psychology*, *51*, 52–66. https://psycnet.apa.org/doi/10.1037/a0038454

Scott, R. M., & Baillargeon, R. (2017). Early false-belief understanding. *Trends in Cognitive Sciences*, *21*, 237–249. https://doi.org/10.1016/j.tics.2017.01.012

Selmeczy, D., & Ghetti, S. (2019). Here is a hint! How children integrate reliable recommendations in their memory decisions. *Journal of Experimental Child Psychology*, *177*, 222–239. https://doi.org/10.1016/j.jecp.2018.08.004

Serpell, R. (2011). Social responsibility as a dimension of intelligence, and as an educational goal: Insights from programmatic research in an African society. *Child Development Perspectives*, *5*, 126–133. https://doi.org/10.1111/j.1750-8606.2011.00167.x

Shultz, S., & Vouloumanos, A. (2010). Three-month-olds prefer speech to other naturally occurring signals. *Language Learning and Development*, *6*(4), 241–257. https://doi.org/10.1080/15475440903507830

Siegel, A. W., & White, S. H. (1982). The child study movement: Early growth and development of the symbolized child. *Advances in Child Development and Behavior*, *17*, 233–285. https://doi.org/10.1016/S0065-2407(08)60361-4

Siegler, R. S. (1991). Strategy choice and strategy discovery. *Learning and Instruction*, *1*, 89–102. https://doi.org/10.1016/0959-4752(91)90020-9

Siegler, R. S. (2005). Children's learning. *American Psychologist*, *60*(8), 769–778. https://doi.org/10.1037/0003-066X.60.8.769

Siegler, R. S. (2006). Microgenetic analysis of learning. In W. Damon (Series Ed.) and D. Kuhn & R. S. Siegler (Vol. Eds.), *Handbook of child psychology: Cognition, perception, and language* (6th ed., Vol. 2, pp. 464–510). New York: Wiley.

Siegler, R. S., & Chen, Z. (2002). Development of rules and strategies: Balancing the old and new. *Journal of Experimental Child Psychology*, *81*, 446–457. https://doi.org/10.1006/jecp.2002.2666

Simons, C., Metzger, S. R., & Sonnenschein, S. (2020). Children's metacognitive knowledge of five key learning processes. *Translational Issues in Psychological Science*, *6*, 32–42. https://psycnet.apa.org/doi/10.1037/tps0000219

Skinner, B. F. (1957). *Verbal behavior*. New York: Appleton-Century-Crofts.

Snow, C. E. (1990). Building memories: The ontogeny of autobiography. In D. Cicchetti & M. Beeghly (Eds.), *The self in transition: Infancy to childhood* (pp. 213–242). Chicago, IL: University of Chicago Press.

Spencer, J. P. (2019). Making sense of developmental dynamics. *Human Development*, *63*, 255–263. https://doi.org/10.1159/000504296

Spencer, J. P., Perone, S., & Buss, A. T. (2011). Twenty years and going strong: A dynamic systems revolution in motor and cognitive development. *Child*

*Development Perspectives*, *5*, 260–266. https://doi.org/10.1111/j.1750-8606 .2011.00194.x

Sperling, G. (1960). The information available in brief visual presentations. *Psychological Monographs*, *74*, 1–29. https://psycnet.apa.org/doi/10.1037/ h0093759

Squire, L. R. (1992). Memory and the hippocampus: A synthesis from findings with rats, monkeys, and humans. *Psychological Review*, *99*(2), 195–231. https://doi.org/10.1037/0033-295X.99.2.195

Sterponi, L. (2010). Learning communicative competence. In D. F. Lancy, J. Bock, & S. Gaskins (Eds.), *The anthropology of learning in childhood* (pp. 235–259). Lanham, MD: Alta Mira Press.

Swain, I. U., Zelazo, P. R., & Clifton, R. K. (1993). Newborn infants' memory for speech sounds retained over 24 hours. *Developmental Psychology*, *29*, 312–323. https://psycnet.apa.org/doi/10.1037/0012-1649.29.2.312

Tabery, J. (2014). *Beyond versus: The struggle to understand the interaction of nature and nurture*. Cambridge, MA: MIT Press.

Tamis-LeMonda, C. S., & Bornstein, M. H. (1989). Habituation and maternal encouragement of attention in infants as predictors of toddler language, play, and representational competence. *Child Development*, *60*, 738–751. https:// psycnet.apa.org/doi/10.2307/1130739

Tamis-LeMonda, C. S., Cristofaro, T. N., Rodriguez, E. T., & Bornstein, M. H. (2006). Early language development: Social influences in the first years of life. In L. Balter & C. S. LeMonda (Eds.), *Child psychology: A handbook of contemporary issues* (2nd ed., pp. 79–108). New York: Psychology Press.

Tardif, T., Shatz, M., & Naigles, L. (1997). Caregiver speech and children's use of nouns versus verbs: A comparison on English, Italian, and Mandarin. *Journal of Child Language*, *24*, 535–565. https://psycnet.apa.org/doi/10 .1017/S030500099700319X

Thelen, E., & Smith, L. B. (2006). Dynamic systems theory. In W. Damon (Series Ed.) and R. M. Lerner (Vol. Ed.), *Handbook of child psychology: Theoretical models of human development* (6th ed., Vol. 1, pp. 258–312). New York: Wiley.

Tomasello, M. (2009). *Why we cooperate*. New York: Bradford.

Tomasello, M. (2016). Cultural learning redux. *Child Development*, *87*, 643–653.

Tomasello, M. (2019). *Becoming human: A theory of ontogeny*. Cambridge, MA: Harvard University Press. https://doi.org/10.4159/9780674988651

Tomasello, M., Carpenter, M., Call, J., Behne, T., & Moll, H. (2005). Understanding and sharing intentions: The origins of cultural cognition. *Behavioral and Brain Sciences*, *28*, 675–735. https://doi.org/10.1017/s0140525x05000129

Tomasello, M., Carpenter, M., & Liszkowski, U. (2007). A new look at infant pointing. *Child Development*, *78*, 705–722. https://doi.org/10.1111/j.1467-8624.2007.01025.x

Tomasello, M., & Farrar, J. (1986). Joint attention and early language. *Child Development*, *57*, 1454–1463. https://psycnet.apa.org/doi/10.2307/1130423

Tõugu, P., Tulviste, T., Schröder, L., Keller, H., & De Geer, B. (2012). Content of maternal open-ended questions and statements in reminiscing with their 4-year-olds: Links with independence and interdependence orientation in European contexts. *Memory*, *20*, 499–510. https://doi.org/10.1080/09658211.2012.683009

Trevarthen, C. (2002). Making sense of infants making sense. *Intellectica*, *34*, 161–188. https://doi.org/10.3406/intel.2002.1078

Trevarthen, C., & Aitken, K. J. (2001). Infant intersubjectivity: Research, theory and clinical applications. *Journal of Child Psychology and Psychiatry*, *42*, 3–48. https://psycnet.apa.org/doi/10.1111/1469-7610.00701

Tronick, E. Z., Als, H., Adamson, L., Wise, S., & Brazelton, T. B. (1978). The infant's response to entrapment between contradictory messages in face-to-face interaction. *Journal of the American Academy of Child Psychiatry*, *17*, 1–13. https://doi.org/10.1016/s0002-7138(09)62273-1

Tulving, E. (1987). Multiple memory systems and consciousness. *Human Neurobiology*, *6*, 67–80. www.proquest.com/scholarly-journals/multiple-memory-systems-consciousness/docview/617445417/se-2?accountid=14521

Turkheimer, E. (2000). Three laws of behavior genetics and what they mean. *Current Directions in Psychological Science*, *9*, 160–164. https://psycnet.apa.org/doi/10.1111/1467-8721.00084

Van Bergen, P., Salmon, K., Dadds, M. R., & Allen, J. (2009). The effects of mother training in emotion-rich, elaborative reminiscing on children's shared recall and emotion knowledge. *Journal of Cognition and Development*, *10* (3), 162–187. https://psycnet.apa.org/doi/10.1080/15248370903155825

van de Vijver, F. J. R., Hofer, J., & Chasiotis, A. (2010). Methodology. In M. H. Bornstein (Ed.), *Handbook of cultural developmental science* (pp. 21–37). New York: Psychology Press.

Van IJzendoorn, M. H., Bakermans-Kranenburg, M. J., Duschinsky, R. et al. (2020). Institutionalisation and deinstitutionalisation of children 1: A systematic and integrative review of evidence regarding effects on development. *The Lancet Psychiatry*, *7*, 703–720. https://doi.org/10.1016/S2215-0366(19)30399-2

Vierkant, T. (2012). Self-knowledge and knowing other minds: The implicit/explicit distinction as a tool in understanding theory of mind. *British Journal of Developmental Psychology*, *30*, 141–155. https://doi.org/10.1111/j.2044-835X.2011.02068.x

Vygotsky, L. S. (1978). *Mind in society: The development of higher mental functions*. Cambridge, MA: Harvard University Press.

Vygotsky, L. S. (1987). *The collected works of L. S. Vygotsky: Problems of general psychology* (Vol. 1). New York: Plenum Press.

Waddington, C. H. (1962). *New patterns in genetics and development*. New York: Columbia University Press.

Waddington, C. H. (1966). *Principles of development and differentiation*. New York: Macmillan.

Wang, Q. (2004). The emergence of cultural self-constructs: Autobiographical memory and self-description in European American and Chinese children. *Developmental Psychology*, *40*, 3–15. https://psycnet.apa.org/doi/10.1037/0012-1649.40.1.3

Wartella, E., Beaudoin-Ryan, L., Blackwell, C. K. et al. (2016). What kind of adults will our children become? The impact of growing up in a media-saturated world. *Journal of Children and Media*, *10*, 13–20. https://doi.org/10.1080/17482798.2015.1124796

Waxman, S. R., Shipley, E. F., & Shepperson, B. (1991). Establishing new subcategories: The role of category labels and existing knowledge. *Child Development*, *62*, 127–138. https://psycnet.apa.org/doi/10.2307/1130709

Weiss, M. J., Zelazo, P. R., & Swain, I. U. (1988). Newborn response to auditory stimulus discrepancy. *Child Development*, 59, 1530–1541. https://psycnet.apa.org/doi/10.2307/1130668

Wellman, H. M. (2006). Theory of mind: A core human cognition. In Q. Jing, M. R. Rosenzweig, G. d'Ydewalle et al. (Eds.), *Progress in psychological science around the world* (pp. 503–525). New York: Psychology Press.

Wellman, H. M. (2017). The development of theory of mind: Historical reflections. *Child Development Perspectives*, *11*, 207–214. https://doi.org/10.1111/cdep.12236

Wentzel, K. R., & Ramani, G. B. (2016). *Handbook of social influences in school contexts: Social-emotional, motivation, and cognitive outcomes*. New York: Taylor & Francis Group.

Werker, J. F., & Desjardins, R. N. (1995). Listening to speech in the first year of life: Experiential influences on phoneme perception. *Current Directions in Psychological Science*, *4*, 76–81. https://psycnet.apa.org/doi/10.1111/1467-8721.ep10772323

Werker, J. F., Pegg, J. E., & McLeod, P. J. (1994). A cross-language investigation of infant preference for infant-directed communication. *Infant Behavior and Development*, *17*, 323–333. https://psycnet.apa.org/doi/10.1016/0163-6383(94)90012-4

Werker, J. F., Pons, F., Dietrich, C. et al. (2007). Infant-directed speech supports phonetic category learning in English and Japanese. *Cognition*, *103*, 147–162. https://doi.org/10.1016/j.cognition.2006.03.006

Werner, J. S., & Siqueland, E. R. (1978). Visual recognition memory in the preterm infant. *Infant Behavior and Development*, *1*, 79–84. https://doi.org/10.1016/S0163-6383(78)80011-3

Wertsch, J. V. (2007). Mediation. In H. Daniels, M. Cole, & J. V. Wertsch (Eds.), *The Cambridge companion to Vygotsky* (pp. 178–192). Cambridge: Cambridge University Press.

Westermann, G., Mareschal, D., Johnson, M. H. et al. (2007). Neuroconstructivism. *Developmental Science*, *10*(1), 75–83. https://doi.org/10.1111/j.1467-7687.2007.00567.x

Wetzel, N., Scharf, F., & Widman, A. (2019). Can't ignore-distraction by task-irrelevant sounds in early and middle childhood. *Child Development*, *90*, 819–830. https://doi.org/10.1111/cdev.13109

Whiting, B. B. (1976). The problem of the packaged variable. In K. F. Riegel & J. A. Meecham (Eds.), *The developing individual in a changing world* (pp. 303–309). Chicago, IL: Aldine.

Willatts, P. (1990). Development of problem solving strategies in infants. In D. F. Bjorklund (Ed.), *Children's strategies* (pp. 23–66). Hillsdale, NJ: Erlbaum.

Willcutt, E. G. (2012). The prevalence of DSM-IV attention-deficit/hyperactivity disorder: A meta-analytic review. *Neurotherapeutics*, *9*, 490–499. https://doi.org/10.1007/s13311-012-0135-8

Wimmer, H., & Perner, J. (1983). Beliefs about beliefs: Representation and constraining function of wrong beliefs in young children's understanding of deception. *Cognition*, *13*, 103–128. https://psycnet.apa.org/doi/10.1016/0010-0277(83)90004-5

Witherington, D. C., & Lickliter, R. (2017). Transcending the nature-nurture debate through epigenetics: Are we there yet? *Human Development*, *60*(2–3), 65–68. https://doi.org/10.1159/000478796

Wood, D., Bruner, J. S., & Ross, G. (1976). The role of tutoring in problem-solving. *Journal of Child Psychology and Psychiatry*, *17*, 89–100. https://psycnet.apa.org/doi/10.1111/j.1469-7610.1976.tb00381.x

Yu, C.-L., Kovelman, I., & Wellman, H. M. (2021). How bilingualism informs theory of mind development. *Child Development Perspectives*, *15*, 154–159. https://doi.org/10.1111/cdep.12412

Zelazo, P. D. (2015). Executive function: Reflection, iterative reprocessing, complexity, and the developing brain. *Developmental Review, 38*, 55–68. https://doi.org/10.1111/cdep.12412

Zelazo, P. D., Blair, C. B., & Willoughby, M. T. (2016). *Executive function: Implications for education (NCER 2017-2000)*. Washington, DC: National Center for Education Research, Institute of Education Sciences, U.S. Department of Education. https://ies.ed.gov/

Zelazo, P. D., Chandler, M., & Crone, E. A. (2010). The birth and early development of a new discipline: Developmental social cognitive neuroscience. In P. D. Zelazo, M. Chandler, & E. Crone (Eds.), *Developmental social cognitive neuroscience* (pp. 3–9). New York: Psychology Press.

Cambridge Elements ⹀

# Child Development

### Marc H. Bornstein
*Eunice Kennedy Shriver National Institute of Child Health and Human Development, Bethesda*
*Institute for Fiscal Studies, London*
*UNICEF, New York City*

Marc H. Bornstein is an Affiliate of the *Eunice Kennedy Shriver* National Institute of Child Health and Human Development, an International Research Fellow at the Institute for Fiscal Studies (London), and UNICEF Senior Advisor for Research for ECD Parenting Programmes. Bornstein is President Emeritus of the Society for Research in Child Development, Editor Emeritus of *Child Development*, and founding Editor of *Parenting: Science and Practice.*

---

### About the Series
Child development is a lively and engaging, yet serious and real-world subject of scientific study that encompasses myriad theories, methods, substantive areas, and applied concerns. Cambridge Elements in Child Development addresses many contemporary topics in child development with unique, comprehensive, and state-of-the-art treatments of principal issues, primary currents of thinking, original perspectives, and empirical contributions to understanding early human development.

# Cambridge Elements ≡

# Child Development

## Elements in the Series

A full series listing is available at: www.cambridge.org/EICD

Printed in the United States
by Baker & Taylor Publisher Services